Japanese For Beginners Phrasebook

Learn The Most Frequently Used Phrases, Expressions, And Vocabulary Words For Travelers And Enthusiasts

Arakaki Saburo

Table Of Content

Introduction

This phrasebook is aimed at new Japanese learners keen on picking up the basics of the language.

Many people are interested in learning Japanese but are often put off due to the complex way in which the language is portrayed to absolute beginners.

I have gone through many materials for beginners but always found myself on the other side of the stick. Why, you may ask?

Many of the learning guides out there focus on grammatical rules and lexicons, which, more often than not, are too confusing and of putting for beginners to grasp and comprehend.

Think back to the time you learned the English language. How did you learn?

You learned through words, broken sentences, and then eventually entire sentences that make complete sense. You learned through listening and memorizing as much vocabulary as possible while vocalizing phrases with your peers and family.

You start by speaking "Cave language," putting together many words that don't make any sense and do not have the correct context, but with more practice and dedication, you become more fluent and proficient in the language.

This is my approach to learning Japanese and any other language. My goal when learning a language is always to pick up the most common words and phrases first and then take it from there. By doing this, your chances of becoming fluent in the language are much higher because you are gradually familiarizing yourself with the sounds of the language. In no time, you will feel confident and assured in your conversation & comprehension ability.

You do not need to have studied any Japanese grammar to benefit from this book; however, it would be better in your favor if you already have a good grasp of the Japanese alphabet.

If, however, you do not know the alphabet yet, that is also fine, as the phrases and words in this book are transliterated, allowing you to follow along in the English language.

I would recommend you pick up the audiobook of this book and follow along so that you can pick up how native Japanese speakers pronounce the words and phrases and so that you may emulate them in the best way possible.

Lastly, please take out a separate notebook and jot down the phrases and vocabulary words you would like to focus on and prioritize first. This phrasebook has over 1400 vocabulary words and phrases, so I recommend you take it slowly at your own pace.

Lastly, remember that repetition is the mother of success, so you will need to listen, write, and constantly repeat to learn effectively and for the long term.

Chapter 1: The Masses

English Phrase	Japanese	Transliteration
Hi there, my name is Hiroko!	やあ、私の名前は弘子です！	Yaa watashi no namae wa hiroko desu!
What is your name?	あなたの名前は何ですか？	Anata no namae wa nandesuka?
I am pleased to meet you!	お会いできて嬉しいです！	Oai dekite ureshii desu!
I don't think we have met before	私たちは以前に会ったことがないと思います	Watashi tachi wa izen ni atta kotoga nai to omoi masu
Good morning	おはよう	ohayou
Good afternoon	こんにちは	Kon-nichi-wa
Good evening	こんばんは	Kon-ban-wa
It was nice seeing you earlier	お会いできてよかったです	Oai dekite yokatta desu
How are you doing?	お元気ですか？	Ogenki desuka?
Where do you live?	どこに住んでいますか？	Doko ni sunde imasu ka?
Where were you born?	出身はどこですか？	Shusshin wa doko desu ka?
How old are you?	何歳ですか？	Nansai desu ka?
Which city do you live in?	どこの街に住んでいますか？	Doko no machi ni sunde imasu ka?
Do you have any siblings?	兄弟はいますか？	Kyoudai wa imasu ka?

English Phrase	Japanese	Transliteration
Goodbye	さようなら	*sayounara*
We should catch up later	後程お会いしましょう	*Nochihodo oai shimashou*
What are you doing in the afternoon?	午後は何をしていますか？	*Gogo wa nani wo shite imasu ka?*
Could you pick me up in the morning?	朝、迎えにきていただけますか？	*Asa mukaeni kite itadakemasu ka?*
Excuse me	すみません	*sumimasen*
I'm sorry I didn't catch your name	すみません、名前をお聞きしていませんでした	*Sumimasen namae wo okiki shite imasen deshita*
Thanks for coming to see me!	会いに来てくれてありがとう！	*Aini kite kurete arigatou !*
I've been meaning to reach out to you	連絡しようと思っていました	*Renraku siyou to omotte imashita*
I missed you	お会いしたかったです	*Oai shitakatta desu*
Are you free for a quick chat?	少しお話しませんか？	*Sukoshi ohanashi shimasen ka?*
I look forward to seeing you again	また会えるのを楽しみにしています	*Mata aeruno wo tanoshimini shite imasu*
How was your journey?	旅行はいかがでしたか？	*Ryokou wa ikaga deshita ka?*
So, what do you do for a living?	ところで、お仕事は何をされているんですか？	*Tokorode oshigoto wa nani wo sarete irundesu ka?*
What are your plans for the future?	将来の夢は何ですか？	*Shourai no yume wa nandesu ka?*

English Phrase	Japanese	Transliteration
What have you been up to lately?	*最近はどうしていましたか？*	*Saikin wa doushite imashita ka?*
Things could be better	あまり良くないです	*Amari yoku nai desu*
Life's good; I can't complain!	*文句なしに良い感じです！*	*Monku nashi ni ii kanji desu!*
I'm not sure about that	*それについてはよく分かりません*	*Soreni tsuite wa yoku wakarimasen*
I couldn't agree more	*大賛成です*	*Daisansei desu*
You've hit the nail on the head there (Expression)	*まさにその通りです*	*Masani sono toori desu*
Leave it to me	*お任せください*	*Omakase kudasai*
Don't worry about it	*それについてはご心配なく*	*Soreni tsuite wa goshinpai naku*
That was really kind of you	*ご親切にありがとうございました*	*Goshinsetsu ni arigatou gozaimashita*
That's a good idea	*良い案ですね*	*Ii an desu ne*
I'm feeling exhausted	*疲れています*	*Tsukarete imasu*
That is really sad to hear!	*それはとても残念です！*	*Soreha totemo zan-nen desu!*
Can you keep it there for me?	*そこに置いておいていただけますか？*	*Sokoni oite oite itadake masu ka?*
It would be awesome if..	*もしそうなら素晴らしいですね*	*Moshi sou nara subarashii desu ne*

English Phrase	Japanese	Transliteration
I'll give you a call later	*後で電話しますね*	*Atode denwa shimasu ne*
How was your weekend?	*週末はいかがでしたか？*	*Shuumatsu wa ikaaga deshita ka?*
What did you get up to this week?	*今週はいかがでしたか？*	*Konshuu wa ikaga deshita ka?*
How are you getting to work?	*通勤はどのようにされていますか？*	*Tsuukin ha donoyouni sarete imasu ka?*
The weather was horrible	*天気は最悪でした*	*Tenki wa saiaku deshita*
I'd rather not comment on that	*それについてはコメントを控えさせてください*	*Soreni tsuite wa komento wo hikaesasete kudasai*
That sounds like a nightmare	*悪夢みたいですね*	*Akumu mitai desu ne*
Take a seat, please	*どうぞお掛けください*	*Douzo okake kudasai*
Would you like Tea/Coffee?	*お茶かコーヒーはいかがですか？*	*Ocha ka ko-hi- wa ikaga desu ka?*
Let me take that for you	*お取りしますね*	*Otori shimasu ne*
I'm relieved to hear that	*そうと聞いて安心しました*	*Souto kiite anshin shimashita*
I'm responsible for this department	*私はこの部門の責任者です*	*Watashi wa kono bumon no sekininsha desu*
How was your flight?	*フライトはいかがでしたか？*	*Furaito wa ikaga deshita ka?*
I don't understand	*理解できません*	*Rikai dekimasen*

English Phrase	Japanese	Transliteration
Could you repeat that again?	もう一度お聞きしてもよろしいですか？	*Mou ichido okiki shitemo yoroshii desu ka?*
I changed my mind	気が変わりました	*Ki ga kawarimashita*
Forget about it	忘れていました	*Wasurete imashita*
Where would I find it?	どこにありますか？	*Doko ni arimasu ka?*
Pardon me; I need to leave	すみません、失礼いたします	*Sumimasen shitsurei itashimasu*
Call me back at another time	また改めてお電話をお願いします	*Mata aratamete odenwa wo onegai shimasu*
I would really appreciate it if you could..	そうしていただけるとありがたいです…	*Soushite itadakeruto arigatai desu*
Could you let him know for me?	彼に伝えていただけますか？	*Kare ni tsutaete itadakemasuka?*
What is your mobile phone number?	携帯電話の番号は何ですか？	*Keitaidenwa no bangou wa nandesu ka?*
How does that sound?	どう思いますか？	*Dou omoimasu ka?*
How can I help you with that?	どのようなご用件でしょうか？	*Donoyouna goyouken deshou ka?*
I'm not in the mood right now	今はそんな気分じゃないです	*Ima wa son-na kibun janai desu*
I'm sorry to bother you	申し訳ございません	*moushiwakegozaimasen*
It's time to leave now	そろそろおいとましますね	*Sorosoro oitoma shimasu ne*

English Phrase	Japanese	Transliteration
I'm a bit busy right now	今はちょっと忙しいです	Imawa chotto isogashii desu
Is it enough for you?	これで十分ですか？	Korede juubun desu ka?
I like your style	気に入りました	Kini-irimashita
I'll think about it	考えておきます	Kangaete okimasu
Never mind	お気になさらず	Okini nasarazu
This is new to me	それは初耳です	Sorewa hatsumimi desu
I don't need anything else from you	もう結構ですよ	Mou kekkou desu yo
Of course, I won't forget	もちろん、忘れません	Mochiron wasuremasen
I love you	愛してる	aishiteru
I hate you	あなたが嫌いです	Anata ga kirai desu
I have a stomach ache	お腹が痛いです	Onaka ga itai desu
I have a headache	頭が痛いです	Atama ga itai desu
He will be here soon	彼はもうすぐ来ますよ	Kare wa mousugu kimasu yo
Let's catch up soon (Expression)	またお会いしましょう	Mata oai shimashou

English Phrase	Japanese	Transliteration
I'll take you up on that offer	お言葉に甘えさせていただきます	*Okotoba ni amaesasete itadakimasu*
Next time	また今度	*Mata kondo*
See you next week	また来週	*Mata raishuu*
What are you up to this weekend?	今週はいかがでしたか？	*Konshuu wa ikaga deshita ka?*
Thank you for your help	お手伝いいただきありがとうございます	*Otetsudai itadaki arigatou gozaimasu*
That's not fair	それは不公平です	*Sorewa fukouhei desu*
I wouldn't recommend that	それはお勧めしません	*Sorewa osusume shimasen*
Get well soon	おだいじに	*odaijini*
How's the family?	ご家族は元気ですか？	*Gokazoku wa genki desuka?*
I liked that	気に入りました	*Kini-irimashita*
I didn't like that	苦手でした	*Nigate deshita*
How were your holidays?	休暇はいかがでしたか？	*Kyuuka wa ikaga deshita ka?*
I like your car!	良い車ですね！	*Ii kuruma desu ne!*
That's such a shame!	それは残念でしたね！	*Sore wa zan-nen deshita ne!*

Chapter 1: Vocabulary

Vocabulary	Japanese	Transliteration
Journey	旅行	*ryokou*
The future	将来	*shourai*
Good	良い	*ii*
Exhausted	疲れた	*tsukareta*
Sad	悲しい	*kanashii*
Idea	案	*An*
Awesome	素晴らしい	*subarashii*
Later	後	*ato*
Weekend	週末	*shuumatsu*
Weather	天気	*tenki*
Horrible	最悪	*saiaku*
Nightmare	悪夢	*akumu*
Tea	お茶	*ocha*
Coffee	コーヒー	*Ko-hi-*

Vocabulary	Japanese	Transliteration
Relieved	安心した	Anshin shita
Responsible	責任者	sekininsha
Department	部門	bumon
Flight	飛行	hikou
Repeat	繰り返す	kurikaesu
Mobile phone number	携帯電話番号	Keitai denwa bangou
Sorry	ごめんなさい	Gomen nasai
Mood	気分	kibun
Time	時間	jikan
Busy	忙しい	isogashii
Style	やり方	yarikata
New	新しい	atarashII
Love	愛	ai
Hate	嫌い	kirai

Vocabulary	Japanese	Transliteration
Stomach ache	腹痛	*fukutsuu*
Headache	頭痛	*zutsuu*
Soon	すぐ	*sugu*
Thank you	ありがとう	*arigatou*
Fair	公平	*kouhei*
Recommend	おすすめ	*osusume*
Help	助ける	*tasukeru*
Family	家族	*kazoku*
Holiday	休日	*kyuujitsu*
Car	車	*kuruma*
Shame	恥	*haji*
City	都市	*toshi*
Big	大きい	*ookii*
Small	小さい	*chiisai*

Chapter 2: At Home

English Phrase	Japanese	Transliteration
Where do you live?	*どこに住んでいますか？*	*Doko ni sunde imasu ka?*
Do you like the city?	*この街は好きですか？*	*Kono machi wa suki desuka?*
Your house is big	*あなたの家は大きいですね*	*Anata no ie wa ookii desu ne*
The carpet is big	*このカーペットは大きいですね*	*Kono ka-petto wa ookii desu ne*
Clean your room!	*部屋を掃除してください！*	*Heya wo souji shite kudasai!*
Can you switch the lights on?	*電気をつけてもらえますか？*	*Denki wo tsukete moraemasu ka?*
Why did you sleep so late?	*どうしてそんなに夜更かしをしたんですか？*	*Doushite son-nani yofukashi wo shitandesu ka?*
What's for breakfast?	*朝ごはんは何ですか？*	*Asagohan wa nandesu ka?*
Could you wash your clothes?	*服を洗濯していただけますか？*	*Fuku wo sentaku shite itadakemasu ka?*
Its bedtime	*寝る時間です*	*Neru jikan desu*
Come downstairs; it's dinner time!	*下に降りてきて。ご飯の時間だよ！*	*Shita ni orite kite gohan no jikan dayo!*
What's on TV tonight?	*今夜のテレビは何？*	*Kon-ya no terebi wa nani?*
It's your turn on the dishes today	*今日はあなたがお皿洗い当番だよ*	*Kyou wa anata ga osara arai touban dayo*
Could you get me a glass of water, son?	*水を一杯もらえるかい？*	*Mizu wo ippai moraeru kai?*

English Phrase	Japanese	Transliteration
The bathroom is occupied	*トイレは使用中です*	*Toire wa shiyouchu desu*
I love cooking	*お料理は大好きです*	*Oryouri wa daisuki desu*
How often do you brush your teeth?	*どれくらいの頻度で歯を磨きますか？*	*Dorekurai no hindo de ha wo migaki masuka?*
Keep your hand away from the stove!	*ストーブには手を触れないで！*	*Suto-bu niwa tewo furenaide!*
What are you cooking today?	*今日は何を料理してるの？*	*Kyou wa nani wo ryouri shiteruno?*
Did you complete your homework?	*宿題は終わらせましたか？*	*Shukudai wa owarase mashita ka?*
Can you hoover the carpets?	*カーペットの掃除をしてもらえますか？*	*Ka-petto no souji wo shite moraemasu ka?*
Can you pass me the TV remote?	*テレビのリモコンを渡してくれる？*	*Terebi no rimokon wo watashite kureru?*
Let's eat dinner together	*一緒に晩ご飯を食べよう！*	*Issho ni bangohan wo tabeyou!*
Your wardrobe is a mess!	*ワードローブがめちゃくちゃです！*	*Wa-doro-bu ga mechakucha desu!*
What are we having for dinner?	*晩ご飯は何を食べましょうか？*	*Bangohan wa naniwo tabemashou ka?*
Don't go to the attic at night	*夜中に屋根裏に行かないでください*	*Yonaka ni yaneura ni ikanaide kudasai*
Do you like the curtains?	*このカーテンは気に入ってる？*	*Kono ka-ten wa kini itteru?*
My siblings were fighting downstairs	*下の階で兄弟が喧嘩をしていた*	*Shita no kai de kyoudai ga kenka wo shiteita*

English Phrase	Japanese	Transliteration
Don't forget to take your key	鍵を忘れないでね	Kagi wo wasurenaide ne
Who is going to lawn the grass?	誰が芝生を敷くつもり？	Dare ga shibafu wo shiku tsumori?
The house caught fire	家が火事になった	Ie ga kaji ni natta
Take your shoes off before entering	入る前に靴を脱いでください	Hairu mae ni kutsu wo nuide kudasai
Where did you park your car?	どこに車を停めましたか？	Doko ni kuruma wo tomemashita ka?
Ring the doorbell before entering	入る前に呼び鈴を鳴らしてください	Hairu mae ni yobirin wo narashite kudasai
Can you open the door quietly, please?	静かにドアを開けていただけますか？	Shizuka ni doa wo akete itadakemasu ka?
Be careful with those wires	線に気を付けてください	Sen ni ki wo tsukete kudasai
Are you walking the dog later?	後で犬の散歩をしますか？	Ato de inu no sanpo wo shimasu ka?
You're late for school, Aiko	遅刻ですよ、愛子	Chikoku desuyo aiko
Don't be late!	遅刻しないで！	Chikoku shinaide!
Who are you walking home with?	誰が家まで一緒に歩いていきますか？	Dare ga ie made issho ni aruite ikimasu ka?
Make sure to pick up your phone when I ring	私が電話したら出るようにしてください	Watashi ga denwa shitara deru youni shite kudasai
Could you wash the dishes?	お皿を洗っていただけますか？	Osara wo aratte itadakemasu ka?

English Phrase	Japanese	Transliteration
Get off the balcony!	*バルコニーから下りなさい！*	*Barukoni- kara orinasai!*
The bathroom is in use	*トイレは使用中です*	*Toire wa shiyouchu desu*
What hair brush do you use?	*どのヘアブラシを使いますか？*	*dono heaburashi wo tsukai masu ka?*
Stop running down the corridor!	*廊下で走るのをやめて！*	*Rouka de hashiruno wo yamete!*
Close the cupboard with you	*食器棚を閉めて*	*Shokkidana wo shimete*
Use the dishwasher	*食洗器を使って*	*Shokusenki wo tsukatte*
We need some new furniture	*何か新しい家具が欲しいね*	*Nanika atarashii kagu ga hoshii ne*
Which floor are you on?	*何階にいるの？*	*Nankai ni iru no?*
Speak to the lady at the desk	*あの席の女性と話してください*	*Ano seki no josei to hanashite kudasai*
Can you cut the grass?	*草刈りをしてもらえる？*	*Kusakari wo shite moraeru?*
The housework is too much for me!	*家事はもうたくさんだ！*	*Kaji wa mou takusan da!*
Could you take the laundry?	*洗濯物を取り込んでくれる？*	*Sentakumono wo torikonde kureru ?*
Where's my pillow?	*私の枕はどこ？*	*Watashi no makura wa doko?*
We need a repair	*修理しなきゃ*	*Shuuri shinakya*

English Phrase	Japanese	Transliteration
Stop jumping on the bed!	*ベッドの上でジャンプしないで！*	*Beddo no ue de janpu shinaide*
Don't leave the tap open	*蛇口を開けたままにしないで*	*Jaguchi wo aketa mama ni shinaide*
Take the rubbish with you on the way out	*ゴミは持っていってね*	*Gomi wa motte ittene*
The wall is being painted	*壁は塗装中です*	*Kabe wa tosouchuu desu*
Close the window for me	*窓をしめてください*	*Mado wo shimete kudasai*
I left it in the refrigerator	*それは冷蔵庫にいれました*	*Sore wa reizouko ni iremashita*
Put that on the bookshelf for me	*それは本棚に置いてください*	*Sore wa hondana ni oite kudasai*
Be careful with that	*気を付けてくださいね*	*Ki wo tsukete kudasai ne*
Drive safely	*安全に運転してね*	*Anzen ni unten shite ne*
How long have you lived here?	*ここにはどれくらい住んでいるんですか？*	*Koko ni wa dorekurai sunde irundesu ka?*
I want to move out	*引っ越したい*	*hikkoshitai*
How many bedrooms do you have?	*寝室はいくつありますか？*	*Shinshitsu wa ikutsu arimasu ka?*
How many washrooms do you have?	*洗面所はいくつありますか？*	*Senmenjo wa ikutsu arimasu ka?*
Watch your head	*頭上に気を付けて*	*Zujou ni ki wo tsukete*

Chapter 2: Vocabulary

Vocabulary	Japanese	Transliteration
Room	*部屋*	*Heya*
Lights	*ライト*	*raito*
Sleep	*眠る*	*nemuru*
Breakfast	*朝食*	*choushoku*
Clothes	*服*	*fuku*
Television	*テレビ*	*terebi*
Dishes	*皿*	*sara*
Glass	*グラス*	*gurasu*
Bathroom	*トイレ*	*toire*
Cooking	*料理*	*ryouri*
Brush	*ブラシ*	*burashi*
Teeth	*歯*	*Ha*
Cooking	*料理*	*ryouri*
Hand	*手*	*te*

Vocabulary	Japanese	Transliteration
Complete	*完了*	*kanryou*
Homework	*宿題*	*shukudai*
Hoover	*掃除機をかける*	*Soujiki wo kakeru*
Carpets	*カーペット*	*Ka-petto*
Remote	*遠隔*	*cnkaku*
Eat	*食べる*	*taberu*
Drink	*飲む*	*nomu*
Dinner	*晩ご飯*	*bangohan*
Together	*一緒*	*issho*
Wardrobc	*ワードローブ*	*Wa-doro-bu*
Attic	*屋根裏部屋*	*yaneurabeya*
Curtains	*カーテン*	*Ka-ten*
Fighting	*喧嘩*	*kenka*
Downstairs	*階下*	*kaika*

Vocabulary	Japanese	Transliteration
Upstairs	*上階*	*joukai*
Key	*鍵*	*kagi*
Grass	*草*	*kusa*
House	*家*	*ie*
Fire	*火*	*hi*
Shoes	*靴*	*kutsu*
Doorbell	*呼び鈴*	*yobirin*
Door	*ドア*	*doa*
Wires	*線*	*sen*
Dog	*犬*	*inu*
School	*学校*	*gakkou*
Late	*遅刻*	*chikoku*
Home	*家*	*ie*
Phone	*電話*	*denwa*

Vocabulary	Japanese	Transliteration
Balcony	*バルコニー*	*Barukoni-*
Hair	*髪*	*kami*
Running	*走っている*	*hashitteiru*
Corridor	*廊下*	*rouka*
Cupboard	*食器棚*	*shokkidana*
Dishwasher	*食洗器*	*shokusenki*
Furniture	*家具*	*kagu*
Floor	*床*	*yuka*
Desk	*机*	*tsukue*
Housework	*家事*	*kaJI*
Laundry	*洗濯*	*sentaku*
Pillow	*枕*	*makura*
Repair	*修理*	*shuuri*
Bed	*ベッド*	*beddo*

Vocabulary	Japanese	Transliteration
Tap	*蛇口*	*jaguchi*
Open	*開く*	*hiraku*
Rubbish	*ゴミ*	*gomi*
Wall	*壁*	*kabe*
Painted	*塗られている*	*nurareteiru*
Window	*窓*	*mado*
Refrigerator	*冷蔵庫*	*reizouko*
Shelf	*棚*	*tana*
Safely	*安全に*	*Anzen ni*
Careful	*気を付けて*	*Ki wo tsukete*
Bedrooms	*寝室*	*shinshitsu*
Washrooms	*洗面所*	*senmenjo*
Head	*頭*	*atama*
Book	*本*	*Hon*

Chapter 3: The Supermarket

English Phrase	Japanese	Transliteration
Where is the frozen section?	*冷凍食品の場所はどこですか？*	*Reitou shokuhin no basho wa doko desu ka?*
Don't forget the milk	*牛乳を忘れないでね*	*Gyu-nyu wo wasurenaide ne*
This till is cash only	*このレジは現金払いのみです*	*Kono reji wa genkin barai nomi desu*
What is wrong with your credit card?	*クレジットカードに何か問題がありますか？*	*Kurejitto ka-do ni nanika mondaiga arimasuka?*
The bread counter is in the next aisle	*パン売り場は隣の通路にあります*	*Pan uriba wa tonari no tsuuro ni arimasu*
The frozen foods are out of date	*この冷凍食品は賞味期限切れです*	*Kono reitou shokuhin wa shoumi kigen gire desu*
Can I have two pounds of fish?	*魚を2ポンドいただけますか？*	*Sakana wo ni pondo itadakemasuka?*
The olives are out of date	*このオリーブは賞味期限切れです*	*Kono ori-bu wa shoumi kigen gire desu*
Where can I find the biscuits?	*ビスケットはどこにありますか？*	*Bisuketto wa doko ni arimasuka?*
Would you like a receipt with that?	*領収書をいただけますか？*	*Ryoushuusho wo itadakemasuka?*
Would you like a bag?	*袋はいりますか？*	*Fukuro wa irimasuka?*
Sorry, this item is currently out of stock	*すみません、こちらは現在品切れです*	*Sumimasen kochirawa genzai shinagire desu*
Where can I find the mayonnaise?	*マヨネーズはどこですか？*	*Mayone-zu wa doko desuka?*
Where can I find the ketchup?	*ケチャップはどこですか？*	*Kechappu wa doko desuka?*

English Phrase	Japanese	Transliteration
Do you accept cash payments?	*現金払いは受け付けていますか？*	*Genkin barai wa uketsukete imasuka?*
Can you bring a loaf of bread with you?	*パンを持ってきてもらえますか？*	*Pan wo mottekite moraemasuka?*
Could you please enter your PIN?	*PINを入力していただけますか？*	*Pin wo nyuuryoku shite itadakemasuka?*
Here's your change, sir	*こちらがお釣りです*	*Kochira ga otsuri desu*
Thank you for shopping with us!	*お買い上げありがとうございます！*	*Okaiage arigatou gozaimasu!*
Where is the dairy milk aisle?	*乳製品売り場はどの通路ですか？*	*Nyuuseihin uriba wa doko desuka?*
Could you tell me the ingredient list?	*成分表を教えていただけますか？*	*Seibunhyou wo oshiete itadakemasuka?*
Are you a vegan?	*あなたはヴィーガンですか？*	*Anata wa vi-gan desuka?*
Where is the toilet?	*トイレはどこですか？*	*Toire wa doko desuka?*
Where are the discounted items?	*割引商品はどこですか？*	*Waribiki shouhin wa dokodesuka?*
The supermarket is busy at this time	*この時間のスーパーマーケットは忙しい*	*Kono jikan no su-pa- ma-ketto wa isogashii*
That parking spot is free	*そこの駐車スペースが空いています*	*Sokono chuusha supe-su ga aite imasu*
That parking spot is taken	*そこの駐車スペースは空いていません*	*Sokono chuusha supe-su wa aite imasen*
You cannot park your car there!	*そこには駐車できません！*	*Sokoniwa chuusha dekimasen!*

English Phrase	Japanese	Transliteration
Can you pass me that, please?	*それを渡していただけますか？*	*Sore wo watashite itadakemasuka?*
I don't drink whole milk	*全乳は飲みません*	*Zennyuu wa nomimasen*
Are these crisps suitable for vegetarians?	*このポテトチップスは菜食主義者に適していますか？*	*Kono potetochippusu wa saishoku shugisha ni tekishite imasuka?*
Where are the disabled toilets?	*身障者用トイレはどこですか？*	*Sinshoushayou toire wa doko desuka?*
The shoplifter got away	*万引きは逃げました*	*Manbiki wa nigemashita*
Is the promotion still on?	*プロモーションはまだ続いていますか？*	*Puromo-shon wa mada tsuzuite imasuka?*
Can you call the sales assistant?	*店員を呼んでいただけますか？*	*Ten-in wo yonde itadakemasuka?*
Check out at the counter, sir	*カウンターをご覧ください*	*Kaunta- wo goran kudasai*
The bananas look ripped	*このバナナは裂けているみたいです*	*Kono banana wa saketeiru mitaidesu*
Do you enjoy a croissant in the morning?	*朝はクロワッサンを食べますか？*	*Asawa kurowassan wo tabemasuka?*
The hair section is that way	*ヘアセクションはあちらです*	*Heasekushon wa achiradesu*
Those sweets will ruin your teeth	*それらのお菓子は歯をダメにする*	*Sorerano okashi wa ha wo dame ni suru*
Don't forget to eat your vegetables!	*野菜を食べるのも忘れずに！*	*Yasai wo taberu nomo wasurezuni!*
Don't fill up your trolley too much	*買い物かごに詰め込みすぎないでね*	*Kaimono kago ni tsumekomi suginaidene*

English Phrase	Japanese	Transliteration
Sorry, sir this section is 18+ only	申し訳ございません、このセクションは18歳以上の方のみご利用いただけます	Moushiwake gozaimasen kono sekushon wa juuhassai ijouno kata nomi goriyou itadakemasu
Do you have your ID with you?	身分証明書はお持ちですか？	Mibun shoumeisho wa omochi desuka?
Security was on high alert	警備は厳戒態勢でした	Keibi wa genkai taisei deshita
Don't forget your receipt, madam	レシートをお忘れなく	Reshi-to wo owasure naku
This coupon has expired	このクーポンは有効期限切れです	Kono ku-pon wa yuukou kigen gire desu
The baby products are over there	ベビー用品はあちらです	Bebi- youhin wa achira desu
I'm looking for potato chips	ポテトチップスをさがしています	Poteto chippusu wo sagashite imasu
How much does this cost?	費用はどれくらいかかりますか？	Hiyou wa dorekurai kakari masuka?
Sorry, we only take cash at the moment	申し訳ございません、現在は現金のみのお取り扱いとなっております	Moushiwake gozaimasen, genzai wa genkin nomino otoriatukai to natteorimasu
Let me check the stock for you	在庫の確認をさせてください	Zaiko no kakunin wo sasete kudasai
No problem, follow me	構いませんよ、こちらへどうぞ	Kamaimasen yo kochira e douzo
Could you help me to self-check out?	セルフレジでの支払いを手伝っていただけませんか？	Serufu reji deno shiharaiwo tetsudatte itadakemasenka?
I would like to form a complaint, please	苦情を入れさせてください	Kujou wo iresasete kudasai
Thank you for shopping with us	お買い上げいただきありがとうございました	Okaiage itadaki arigatou gozaimashita

English Phrase	Japanese	Transliteration
It was a pleasure to help you	*お力添えできて光栄です*	*Ochikarazoe dekite kouei desu*
Could you help me with this?	*これを手伝っていただけませんか？*	*Kore wo tetsudatte itadakemasenka?*
Have a nice day!	*良い一日を！*	*Yoi ichinichi wo!*
How can I assist you today?	*本日はどういったご用件でしょうか？*	*Honjitsu wa douitta goyouken deshouka?*
Can I try it on?	*試着してもいいですか？*	*Shichaku shitemo iidesuka?*
Can you pay for this?	*こちらでお支払いできますか？*	*Kochira de oshiharai dekimasuka?*
I forgot my shopping list at home	*お買い物リストを家に忘れた*	*Okaimono risuto wo ie ni wasureta*
You left the car engine on	*車のエンジンがかけっぱなしですよ*	*Kuruma no enjin ga kakeppanashi desuyo*
Why are the prices so high?	*どうしてこんなに値段が高いんですか？*	*Doushite konnnani nedan ga takaindesuka?*
Do you have a promotion right now?	*おすすめはありますか？*	*Osusume wa arimasuka?*
Are there any student discounts?	*学割はありますか？*	*Gakuwari wa arimasuka?*
Could you patiently wait in the queue, please?	*順番をお待ちいただいてもよろしいでしょうか？*	*Junban wo omachi Itadaitemo yorosii deshouka?*
Why is the line so long?!	*どうしてこんなに列が長いんだ！？*	*Doushite konnnani retsuga nagainda!?*
Let's come back at another time	*また今度来よう*	*Mata kondo koyou*

English Phrase	Japanese	Transliteration
What is your return policy?	返品条件を教えていただけますか？	*Henpin jouken wo oshiete itadakemasuka?*
Do you have any more stock at the back?	もっと在庫はありませんか？	*Motto zaiko wa arimasenka?*
These trousers are available online	このズボンはオンラインでご購入いただけます	*Kono zubon wa onrain de gokounyuu itadakemasu*
No more candy for you!	もう飴はあげません！	*Mou ame wa agemasen!*
This is a bargain!	これはお買い得です！	*Kore wa okaidoku desu!*
Is there another size available?	別のサイズはありますか？	*Betsu no saizu wa arimasuka?*
Are these items refundable?	返金は可能ですか？	*Henpin wa kanou desuka?*
Can I change my appointment?	予定を変更できますか？	*Yotei wo henkou dekimasuka?*
Are these bananas free trade	このバナナは自由貿易ですか？	*Kono banana wa jiyuu boueki desuka?*
That section is unhealthy	そのセクションは不健康です	*Sono sekushon wa fukenkou desu*
I am currently on a diet	今はダイエット中です	*Ima wa daietto chuu desu*
The carbohydrates in this are too much!	炭水化物が多すぎます！	*Tansuikabutsu ga oosugimasu!*
Where is the cereal section?	シリアル売り場はどこですか？	*Siriaru uriba wa doko desuka?*
Can I buy this item in bulk?	これはまとめて買えますか？	*Kore wa matomete kaemasuka?*

English Phrase	Japanese	Transliteration
I love that dress	このドレスいいですね	Kono doresu iidesune
Can we come back another time?	また改めて来てもいいですか？	Mata aratamete kitemo iidesuka?
What time does the store close?	閉店時間は何時ですか？	Heiten jikan wa nanji desuka?
Where did you buy those from?	これはどこから仕入れたんですか？	Kore wa dokokara shiiretandesuka?
Can we gift-wrap these, please?	包装していただいてもいいですか？	Houshou shite itadaitemo iidesuka?
Your Shopping basket is full	買い物かごがいっぱいですよ	Kaimonokago ga ippai desuyo
Excuse me; I'm looking for...	すみません、...をさがしているんですが	Sumimasen, ... wo sagashite irundesuga
What time do you close on Sundays?	日曜日は何時に閉店しますか？	Nichiyoubi wa nanji ni heiten shimasuka?
Are these items reduced to clear?	これらはおつとめ品ですか？	Korera aw otsutome hin desuka?
I left my wallet at home!	家に財布を忘れた！	Ieni saifu wo wasureta!
Don't forget the trolley at the door	入り口付近の買い物かごのカートをお忘れなく	Iriguchi fukin no kaimonokago no ka-to wo owasurenaku
Where is the bookstore?	本屋はどこですか？	Hon-ya wa dokodesuka?
Can you recommend something for me?	何かおすすめはありますか？	Nanika osusume wa arimasuka?
We're open from 9 to 5	9時から5時まで営業しています	Kuji kara goji made eigyou shiteimasu

Chapter 3: Vocabulary

Vocabulary	Japanese	Transliteration
Frozen	冷凍	*Reitou*
Section	セクション	*sekushon*
Milk	牛乳	*gyuunyuu*
Till	レジ	*reji*
Cash	現金	*genkin*
Credit card	クレジットカード	*Kurejittoka-do*
Bread	パン	*pan*
Counter	カウンター	*Kaunta-*
Aisle	通路	*tsuuro*
Out of date	賞味期限切れ	*Shoumi kigen gire*
Pounds	ポンド	*pondo*
Fish	魚	*sakana*
Olives	オリーブ	*Ori-bu*
Biscuits	ビスケット	*bisuketto*

Vocabulary	Japanese	Transliteration
Receipt	*レシート*	*Reshi-to*
Bag	*袋*	*fukuro*
Item	*商品*	*shouhin*
Mayonnaise	*マヨネーズ*	*Mayone-zu*
Ketchup	*ケチャップ*	*kechappu*
Payments	*支払い*	*shiharai*
Loaf	*パン*	*pan*
PIN	*ピン*	*pin*
Shopping	*お買い物*	*okaimono*
Dairy milk	*全乳*	*zennnyuu*
Ingredient	*材料*	*zairyou*
Vegan	*ヴィーガン*	*vi-gan*
Toilet	*トイレ*	*toire*
Discounted	*割引*	*waribiki*

Vocabulary	Japanese	Transliteration
Supermarket	*スーパーマーケット*	*Su-pa-ma-ketto*
Parking	*駐車場*	*chuushajou*
Spot	*場所*	*basho*
Free	*空いている*	*aiteiru*
Taken	*取られている*	*torareteiru*
Vegetarians	*ベジタリアン*	*bejitarian*
Disabled toilets	*身障者用トイレ*	*Sinshoushayou toire*
Shoplifter	*万引き*	*manbiki*
Promotion	*プロモーション*	*Puromo-shon*
Sales Assistant	*店員*	*Ten-in*
Counter	*カウンター*	*Kaunta-*
Bananas	*バナナ*	*banana*
Ripped	*裂けている*	*saketeiru*
Croissant	*クロワッサン*	*kurowassan*

Vocabulary	Japanese	Transliteration
Sweets	*お菓子*	*okashi*
Ruin	*ダメにする*	*damenisuru*
Vegetables	*野菜*	*yasai*
Trolley	*トロリー*	*Torori-*
ID	*身分証明書*	*Mibun shoumei sho*
Security	*警備*	*keibi*
Alert	*警戒*	*keikai*
Coupon	*クーポン*	*Ku-pon*
Products	*商品*	*shouhin*
Potato	*じゃがいも*	*jagaimo*
Cost	*費用*	*hiyou*
Stock	*在庫*	*zaiko*
Self-checkout	*セルフレジ*	*serufureji*
Complaint	*苦情*	*kujou*

Vocabulary	Japanese	Transliteration
Pleasure	喜び	*yorokobi*
Nice	良い	*ii*
Assist	手伝う	*tetsudau*
Try	試す	*tamesu*
Pay	支払い	*shiharai*
List	リスト	*risuto*
Engine	エンジン	*enjin*
Prices	値段	*Nedan*
High	高い	*takai*
Low	低い	*hikui*
Student discount	学割	*gakuwari*
Queue	順番	*junban*
Line	列	*retsu*
Return policy	返品条件	*Henpin jouken*

Vocabulary	Japanese	Transliteration
Trousers	*ズボン*	*zubon*
Available	*利用可能*	*Riyou kanou*
Online	*オンライン*	*onrain*
Candy	*飴*	*ame*
Bargain	*安売り*	*Yasu uri*
Size	*大きさ*	*ookisa*
Refundable	*返金可能*	*Henpin kanou*
Appointment	*予定*	*yotei*
Unhealthy	*不健康*	*fukenkou*
Healthy	*健康*	*kenkou*
Diet	*ダイエット*	*daietto*
Carbohydrates	*炭水化物*	*tansuikabutsu*
Cereal	*シリアル*	*shiriaru*
Bulk	*バルク*	*baruku*

Vocabulary	Japanese	Transliteration
Dress	*ドレス*	*doresu*
Gift	*贈り物*	*okurimono*
Wrap	*包装*	*housou*
Full	*満杯*	*manpai*
Empty	*空*	*kara*
Basket	*かご*	*kago*
Wallet	*財布*	*saifu*
Bookstore	*本屋*	*Hon-ya*

Chapter 4: Public transport

English Phrase	Japanese	Transliteration
Where can I buy my ticket?	切符はどこで買えますか？	*Kippu wa doko de kaemasuka?*
Do you know where the ticket office is?	切符売り場はどこですか？	*Kippu uriba wa doko desuka?*
How much is a single ticket?	片道切符はいくらですか？	*Katamichi kippu wa ikura desuka?*
How much is a return ticket?	往復切符はいくらですか？	*Oufuku kippu wa ikura desuka?*
Which zones does the train travel in?	この列車はどの区間を走行しますか？	*Kono ressha wa dono kukan wo soukou shimasuka?*
Excuse me, how many stops until we arrive?	すみません、到着までいくつの駅に止まりますか？	*Sumimasen, touchaku made ikutsu no eki ni tomarimasuka?*
I'm getting off here	私はここで降ります	*Watashi wa koko de orimasu*
I've lost my ticket, unfortunately	残念ながら、切符をなくしました	*Zannen nagara, kippu wo nakushimashita*
The train terminates at the next station	次の駅で終点です	*Tsugi no eki de shuuten desu*
The next station is my stop	次が私の降りる駅です	*Tsugi ga watashi no oriru eki desu*
Where do the taxis stop?	タクシーはどこに止まりますか？	*Takushi- wa doko ni tomarimasuka?*
Please don't forget your belongings	持ち物を忘れないでください	*Mochimono wo wasurenaide kudasai*
Please mind the gap	足元の隙間にご注意ください	*Ashimoto no sukimas ni gochuui kudasai*
I missed my bus!	バスを逃した！	*Basu wo nogashita!*

English Phrase	Japanese	Transliteration
I would like to buy a travel card, please	トラベルカードを一枚ください	*Toraberu ka-do wo ichimai kudasai*
Could you open the window, please?	窓を開けていただけますか？	*Mado wo akete itadakemasuka?*
Where can I find lost property?	遺失物はどこで見つけられますか？	*Ishitsubutsu wa doko de mitsukeraremasuka?*
What time is the bus departing?	バスは何時に発車しますか？	*Basu wa nanji ni hassha shimasuka?*
What time is the bus arriving?	バスの到着時刻はいつですか？	*Basu no touchaku jikoku wa itsudesuka?*
Don't travel at peak hours!	ピーク時に旅行しないで！	*Pi-ku ji ni ryokou shinaide!*
The underground is undergoing a planned closure	地下は計画的に閉鎖を行っています	*Chika wa keikakuteki ni heisa wo okonatte imasu*
Where can we buy a group ticket?	グループチケットはどこで買えますか？	*Guru-pu chiketto wa dokode kaemasuka?*
Can I have a one-way ticket, please?	片道切符を一枚いただけますか？	*Katamichi kippu wo ichimai itadakemasuka?*
I booked the wrong ticket by accident	間違えて誤った切符を予約してしまいました	*Machigaete ayamatta kippu wo yoyaku shite shimaimashita*
Can I change my ticket?	切符を変更できますか？	*Kippu wo henkou dekimasuka?*
The bus is coming in 30 minutes	バスは30分以内に到着します	*Basu wa sanjuppun inai ni touchaku shimasu*
The train station is crowded	駅は混んでいます	*Eki wa konde imasu*
The train was delayed	電車は遅れています	*Densha wa okurete imasu*

English Phrase	Japanese	Transliteration
Please check in here	こちらでチェックインしてください	*Kochira de chekkuin shitekudasai*
Your passport has expired	あなたのパスポートは期限切れです	*Anatano pasupo-to wa kigen gire desu*
The flight is taking off shortly	飛行機は間もなく離陸します	*Hikouki wa mamonaku ririku shimasu*
The flight has been delayed	飛行機は遅れています	*Hikouki wa okurete imasu*
Boarding control is that way	出入国管理はあちらです	*Shutunyuukoku kanri wa achira desu*
Where can I weigh the bags?	バッグの重量はどこで量りますか？	*Bagguno juuryou wa dokode hakarimasuka?*
Please do not leave any bags unattended	荷物は放置しないでください	*Nimotsu wa houchi shinaide kudasai*
Could I see your passport, please?	パスポートを見せてください	*Pasupo-to wo misete kudasai*
Your gate is on the other side	あなたのゲートは向こう側です	*Anata no ge-to wa mukougawa desu*
When will I receive my boarding pass?	いつ搭乗券を受け取れますか？	*Itsu toujouken wo uketoremasuka?*
What is your ticket number?	チケットの番号は何番ですか？	*Chiketto no bangou wa nanban desuka?*
What is your booking reference?	予約番号は何番ですか？	*Yoyaku bangou wa nanban desuka?*
How many pieces of luggage do you have?	荷物はいくつありますか？	*Nimotsu wa ikutsu arimasuka?*
We wish you a pleasant flight	快適な空の旅をお祈りします	*Kaiteki na sora no tabi wo oinori shimasu*

English Phrase	Japanese	Transliteration
The bus is running late	*バスは遅延しています*	*Basu wa chien shiteimasu*
Please show your ticket	*チケットを見せてください*	*Chiketto wo misete kudasai*
The gate is opening shortly	*ゲートは間もなく開きます*	*Ge-to wa mamonaku hirakimasu*
The gate has just closed	*ゲートはたった今閉まりました*	*Ge-to wa tattaima shimarimashita*
What is your flight number?	*便名は何ですか？*	*Binmei wa nandesuka?*
Please fasten your seatbelt	*シートベルトを締めてください*	*Si-toberuto wo shimete kudasai*
The bus is full	*バスは満員です*	*Basu wa man-in desu*
Please wait for the next bus	*次のバスをお待ちください*	*Tsugi no basu wo omachi kudasai*
Where is the bus schedule?	*バスの時刻表はどこですか？*	*Basu no jikokuhyou wa dokodesuka?*
Do you have a map?	*地図をお持ちですか？*	*Chizu wo omochi desuka?*
There was an accident on road	*交通事故がありました*	*Koutsuu jiko ga arimashita*
Will you tip me?	*チップをいただけますか？*	*Chippu wo itadakemasuka?*
Please prepare for take-off	*離陸の準備をしてください*	*Ririku no junbi wo shitekudasai*
Please prepare for landing	*着陸の準備をしてください*	*Chakuriku no junbi wo shitekudasai*

Chapter 4: Vocabulary

Vocabulary	Japanese	Transliteration
Ticket	切符	*kippu*
Office	オフィス	*ofisu*
Travel	旅行	*ryokou*
Zone	区域	*kuiki*
Travel	旅行	*ryokou*
Taxi	タクシー	*Takushi-*
Belongings	持ち物	*mochimono*
Gap	隙間	*sukima*
Bus	バス	*basu*
Travel card	トラベルカード	*Toraberuka-do*
Property	財産	*zaisan*
Departure	出発	*shuppatsu*
Arrival	到着	*touchaku*
Peak hours	ピーク時	*Pi-kuji*

Vocabulary	Japanese	Transliteration
The underground	地下	*chika*
Closure	閉鎖	*heisa*
Booking	予約	*yoyaku*
Crowded	混んでいる	*kondeiru*
Delayed	遅れている	*okureteiru*
Passport	パスポート	*Pasupo-to*
Expired	期限切れ	*kigengire*
Flight	フライト	*furaito*
Take off	離陸	*ririku*
Boarding control	出入国管理	*shutsunyuuryokukanri*
Unattended	無人	*mujin*
Gate	ゲート	*Ge-to*
Booking reference	予約番号	*yoyakubangou*
Luggage	荷物	*nimotsu*

Vocabulary	Japanese	Transliteration
Seatbelt	*シートベルト*	*Shi-toberuto*
Schedule	*スケジュール*	*Sukeju-ru*
Map	*地図*	*chizu*
Accident	*事故*	*jiko*
Road	*道*	*michi*
Tip	*チップ*	*chippu*

Chapter 5: School/University

English Phrase	Japanese	Transliteration
Good morning	*おはようございます*	*Ohayou gozaimasu*
Good afternoon students	*こんにちは皆さん*	*Kon-nichiwa minasan*
How are you feeling today?	*調子はどうですか？*	*Choushi wa doudesuka?*
Shall we take the register?	*出席を取ります*	*Shusseki wo torimasu*
Let's begin the lesson	*授業を始めましょう*	*Jugyou wo hajimemashou*
Please don't interrupt me when I am speaking!	*私が話している時は遮らないでください！*	*Watashi ga hanashiteiru toki wa saegiranaide kudasai!*
Who has prepared the homework?	*宿題は誰が用意しましたか？*	*Shukudai wa darega youi shimashitaka?*
Why are you late for class?	*なぜ授業に遅れたんですか？*	*Naze jugyou ni okuratandesuka?*
Please put your books away	*本を仕舞ってください*	*Hon wo shimatte kudasai*
Don't forget your homework	*宿題を忘れないでください*	*Shukudai wo wasurenaide kudasai*
Prepare the next section for the next class	*次の授業のために次のセクションの準備をしてください*	*Tsugi no jugyou notame ni tsugi no sekushon no junbi wo shite kudasai*
Where have you been?!	*どこに行っていたんですか？！*	*Doko ni itte itandesuka!?*
Please wait a moment	*ちょっと待ってください*	*Chotto matte kudasai*
Everyone back to their seats, please	*皆さん、席に戻ってください*	*Minasan, seki ni modotte kudasai*

English Phrase	Japanese	Transliteration
How was the half-term break?	*中休みはいかがでしたか？*	*Nakayasumi wa ikaga deshitaka?*
Enjoy your weekend, students!	*週末を楽しんでくださいね！*	*Shuumatsu wo tanoshinde kudasaine!*
Why did you not do the homework?	*なぜ宿題をやらなかったんですか？*	*Naze shukudai wo yaranakattandesuka?*
Open your books to page 5	*5ページを開いてください*	*Gope-ji wo hiraite kudasai*
Could you all get into groups of three?	*三人一組に分かれてください*	*San-nin hitokumi ni wakarete kudasai*
Please raise your hand if you want to answer a question	*問題に答えたければ手をあげてください*	*Mondai ni kotaetakereba te wo agete kudasai*
Who would like to answer the next question?	*次の問題に答えたい人はいますか？*	*Tsugi no mondai ni kotaetai hito wa imasuka?*
Raise your voice, so we can hear you	*聞こえるように大きい声でお願いします*	*Kikoeru youni ookii koede onegai shimasu*
It's your turn to read	*あなたが読む番です*	*Anata ga yomu ban desu*
Finish this activity at home	*この活動は家で終わらせてください*	*Kono katsudou wa ie de owarasete kudasai*
What page did we finish on?	*どのページで終わっていましたか？*	*Dono pe-ji de owatte imashitaka?*
Can somebody pull down the blinds?	*誰かブラインドを下げてくれませんか？*	*Dare ka buraindo wo sagete kuremasenka?*
I'm sorry for being so late	*遅れてごめんなさい*	*Okurete gomen nasai*
Your attendance is poor this week	*あなたの今週の出席率は低いですね*	*Anata no konshuu no shussekiritsu wa hikui desune*

English Phrase	Japanese	Transliteration
Get out of my classroom!	*教室から出ていきなさい！*	*Kyoushitsu kara dete ikinasai!*
Can you repeat that again, sir?	*もう一度言っていただけますか？*	*Mou ichido itte itadakemasuka?*
You will receive your results next week	*結果は来週受け取れます*	*Kekka wa raishuu uketoremasu*
Can I go to the toilet, please?	*トイレに行っていいですか？*	*Toire ni itte iidesuka?*
You will sit in detention	*あなたは居残りです*	*Anata wa inokori desu*
Can somebody pull up the blinds?	*誰かブラインドをあげてもらえますか？*	*Dareka buraindo wo agete moraemasuka?*
Where is the class timetable?	*時間割はどこですか？*	*Jikanwari wa doko desuka?*
Please bring your textbooks next week	*来週は教科書を持ってきてください*	*Raishuu wa kyoukasho wo mottekite kudasai*
How did you get to that answer?	*どうやってその解答に辿り着きましたか？*	*Douyatte sono kaitou ni tadoritsuki mashitaka?*
What did you learn from class yesterday?	*昨日の授業から何を学んだんですか？*	*Kinou no jugyou kara nani wo manandandesuka?*
I'm not so good at mathematics	*数学はあまり得意ではないです*	*Suugaku wa amari tokui dewa naidesu*
I'm really good at sciences	*科学はすごく得意です*	*Kagaku wa sugoku tokui desu*
English is my favorite subject	*英語はお気に入りの教科です*	*Eigo wa okiniiri no kyouka desu*
I passed my science exam!	*科学の試験に合格しました！*	*Kagaku no shiken ni goukaku shimashita!*

English Phrase	Japanese	Transliteration
I need help with the homework	宿題を手伝ってほしいです	*Shukudai wo tetsudatte hoshii desu*
What are you doing after school?	放課後は何をしていますか？	*Houkago wa nani wo shite imasuka?*
How are you getting home?	どうやって帰宅していますか？	*Douyatte kitaku shite imasuka?*
Would you sit with me during lunch break?	お昼休みは一緒に座りませんか？	*Ohiruyasumi wa issho ni suwari masenka?*
I forgot my lunch at home	お昼ご飯を家に忘れた	*Ohiru gohan wo ie ni wasureta*
What is your favorite subject?	お気に入りの教科は何ですか？	*Okiniiri no kyouka wa nandesuka?*
Did you read this textbook?	教科書は読みましたか？	*Kyoukasho wa yomimashitaka?*
Can I borrow your pencil?	鉛筆を借りてもいいですか？	*Enpitsu wo karitemo iidesuka?*
Can I borrow your ruler?	定規を借りてもいいですか？	*Jougi wo karitemo iidesuka?*
Can I borrow your rubber?	消しゴムを借りてもいいですか？	*Keshigomu wo karitemo iidesuka?*
Speak to me after the class	授業の後に話しかけてください	*Jugyou no ato ni hanashikakete kudasai*
Let's take the register	出席を取りましょう	*Shusseki wo torimashou*
I will take your questions afterward	質問はこの後受け付けます	*Shitsumon wa kono ato uketsukemasu*
Did you understand that concept?	その概念は理解できましたか？	*Sono gainen wa rikai dekimashitaka?*

English Phrase	Japanese	Transliteration
I need help with the homework	*宿題を手伝ってほしいです*	*Shukudai wo tetsudatte hoshii desu*
What are you doing after school?	*放課後は何をしていますか？*	*Houkago wa nani wo shite imasuka?*
How are you getting home?	*どうやって帰宅していますか？*	*Douyatte kitaku shite imasuka?*
Would you sit with me during lunch break?	*お昼休みは一緒に座りませんか？*	*Ohiruyasumi wa issho ni suwari masenka?*
I forgot my lunch at home	*お昼ご飯を家に忘れた*	*Ohiru gohan wo ie ni wasureta*
What is your favorite subject?	*お気に入りの教科は何ですか？*	*Okiniiri no kyouka wa nandesuka?*
Did you read this textbook?	*教科書は読みましたか？*	*Kyoukasho wa yomimashitaka?*
Can I borrow your pencil?	*鉛筆を借りてもいいですか？*	*Enpitsu wo karitemo iidesuka?*
Can I borrow your ruler?	*定規を借りてもいいですか？*	*Jougi wo karitemo iidesuka?*
Can I borrow your rubber?	*消しゴムを借りてもいいですか？*	*Keshigomu wo karitemo iidesuka?*
Speak to me after the class	*授業の後に話しかけてください*	*Jugyou no ato ni hanashikakete kudasai*
Let's take the register	*出席を取りましょう*	*Shusseki wo torimashou*
I will take your questions afterward	*質問はこの後受け付けます*	*Shitsumon wa kono ato uketsukemasu*
Did you understand that concept?	*その概念は理解できましたか？*	*Sono gainen wa rikai dekimashitaka?*

English Phrase	Japanese	Transliteration
Please switch off your mobile phone when you come to class	*授業中は携帯電話を切ってください*	*Jugyouchuu wa keitai denwa wo kitte kudasai*
Have you prepared for your exam?	*試験の準備はしてきましたか？*	*Shiken no junbi wa shitekimashitaka?*
Please switch off the Air conditioning	*エアコンを切ってください*	*Eakon wo kitte kudasai*
Don't make up any excuses!	*言い訳をしないでください！*	*Iiwake wo shinaide kudasai*
I am nervous in class	*授業中はそわそわする*	*Jugyouchuu wa sowasowa suru*
You are easily distracted by your friends	*あなたは友達に気を取られやすい*	*Anata wa tomodachi ni ki wo torareyasui*
Your work ethic is poor	*意欲的ではないようですね*	*Iyokuteki dewa nai youdesune*
What do you eat at lunchtime?	*お昼は何を食べますか？*	*Ohiru wa nani wo tabemasuka?*
Do you eat at the school cafeteria?	*カフェテリアで食べますか？*	*Kafeteria de tabemasuka?*
Don't leave the classroom until the bell rings!	*ベルが鳴る前に教室から出ないでください！*	*Beru ga naru mae ni kyoushitsu kara denaide kudasai!*
When is graduation?	*卒業はいつ？*	*Sotsugyou wa itsu?*
What do you study?	*何を勉強したの？*	*Nani wo benkyou shitano?*
What does your course consist of?	*コースはどのような構成ですか？*	*Ko-su wa donoyouna kousei desuka?*
The lecturer is ill today	*講師は本日病欠です*	*Koushi wa honjitsu byouketsu desu*

English Phrase	Japanese	Transliteration
School has been canceled	*学校は休みになりました*	*Gakkou wa yasumi ni narimashita*
What are your plans after you finish school?	*卒業したらどうするの？*	*Sotsugyou shitara dousuruno?*
I'm in my first year of university	*大学一年生です*	*Daigaku ichinensei desu*
I hate my school	*学校が嫌いです*	*Gakkou ga kirai desu*
What is your least favorite subject?	*一番嫌いな科目は何ですか？*	*Ichiban kiraina kamoku wa nandesuka?*
What did you think of the lesson?	*レッスンについてどう思った？*	*Ressun ni tsuite dou omotta?*
What did you think of the class?	*授業についてどう思った？*	*Jugyou ni tsuite dou omotta?*
Today is presentation day!	*本日はプレゼンテーションの日です！*	*Honjitsu wa purezente-shon no hi desu!*
Keep your attention on me!	*私に注目してください！*	*Watashi ni chuumoku shitekudasai!*
Did you pass your exam?	*試験は合格した？*	*Shiken wa goukaku shita?*
Did you fail your exam?	*試験に落ちた？*	*Shiken ni ochita?*
I'll catch up with you later	*後で連絡するね*	*Ato de renraku surune*
These subjects are compulsory	*これらの科目は必修です*	*Korera no kamoku wa hisshuu desu*
What did you choose for your optional modules?	*追加科目は何を選びましたか？*	*Tsuika kamoku wa nani wo erabimashitaka?*

English Phrase	Japanese	Transliteration
I study at that faculty	その学部で勉強します	Sono gakubu de benkyou shimasu
What are the entry requirements there?	入学の条件は何ですか？	Nyuugaku no jouken wa nandesuka?
Have you paid your tuition fees?	学費は支払いましたか？	Gakuhi wa shiharai mashitaka?
I graduated with a major!	専攻を卒業しました！	Senkou wo sotsugyou shimashita!
Are you coming in for parent's evening?	保護者会には来ますか？	Hogoshakai niwa kimasuka?
Did you get your certificate?	証書は受け取りましたか？	Shousho wa uketori mashitaka?
The academic year is coming to an end	今年度は終了しました	Kon-nendo wa shuuryou shimashita
Which accommodation are you staying at?	どの寮に泊まっていますか？	Dono ryou ni tomatte imasuka?
Are you a part-time student?	定時制の学生ですか？	Teijisei no gakusei desuka?
Are you a full-time student?	全日制の学生ですか？	Zen nichisei no gakusei desuka?
What's your roommate like?	ルームメイトはどんな人ですか？	Ru-mumeito wa donna hito desuka?
I missed the deadline for application	申込期限を過ぎてしまった	Moushikomi kigen wo sugite shimatta
Are you self-funded?	自己資金ですか？	Jikoshikin desuka?
Did you take out a university loan?	学生ローンを受けていますか？	Gakusei ro-n wo ukete imasuka?

English Phrase	**Japanese**	**Transliteration**
The workload is too much for me!	*仕事量が多すぎる！*	*Shigotoryou ga oosugiru!*
Can you save me a seat on the bus?	*バスの席を取っておいてくれる？*	*Basu no seki wo totte oite kureru?*
I applied for the scholarship	*奨学金を申し込みました*	*Shougakukin moushikomi mashita*
The project was submitted last minute	*プロジェクトは最後の1分で申し込まれました*	*Purojekuto wa saigo no ippun de moushikomare mashita*
Are you doing any additional research at home?	*自宅で追加の調査をしていますか？*	*Jitaku de tsuika no chousa wo shiteimasuka?*
Do you have a curriculum vitae?	*履歴書は持っていますか？*	*Rirekisho wa motte imasuka?*
I am meeting with my supervisor later	*後で教科主任に会う予定です*	*Atode kyoukashunin ni au yotei desu*
Come see me in my office	*私のオフィスまで来てください*	*Watashi no ofisu made kite kudasai*
I am looking for one-to-one support	*一対一のサポートを探しています*	*Ittai ichi no sapo-to wo sagashite imasu*
How can I further improve my grade?	*どうすればさらに成績を上げられるでしょうか？*	*Dousureba sarani seiseki wo agerareru deshouka?*
What are your career plans?	*あなたのキャリアプランは何ですか？*	*Anata no kyaria puran wa nandesuka?*
Is this your field of expertise?	*これがあなたの専門分野ですか？*	*Korega anata no sennmon bun-ya desuka?*
I am now qualified	*これで私は有資格者です*	*Kore de watashi wa yuushikakusha desu*
I enjoy the topic of discussion	*ディスカッションの話題を楽しんでいます*	*Disukasshon no wadai wo tanoshinde imasu*

English Phrase	Japanese	Transliteration
Speak to a member of staff	職員と話してください	*Shokuin to hanashite kudasai*
What time do you finish school?	何時に学校が終わりますか？	*Nanji ni gakkou ga owarimasuka?*
Let's walk home together	一緒に歩いて帰ろう	*Issho ni aruite kaerou*
Are you applying for an apprenticeship`?	アプレンティスシップには申し込んでる？	*Apurentisu shippu niwa moushikonderu?*
I didn't attend much this semester	今学期はあまり出席しなかった	*Kongakki wa amari shusseki shinakatta*
Are you coming on the school trip?	修学旅行には来る？	*Shuugaku ryokou niwa kuru?*
I finished my assignment	宿題が終わりました	*Shukudai ga owari mashita*
Did you apply for the bursary?	奨学金は申し込みましたか？	*Shougakukin wa moushikomi mashitaka?*
The student dormitory is bad	あの学生寮は悪い	*Ano gakuseiryou wa warui*
You should enroll in extra curriculum classes	追加科目を登録してください	*Tsuika kamoku wo touroku shitekudasai*
Did you memorize the notes?	注意書きは覚えましたか？	*Chuuigaki wa oboe mashitaka?*
I hope to see you around	お会いできるのを楽しみにしています	*Oai dekiru nowo tanoshimini shiteimasu*
Could you close the window, please?	窓を閉めていただけますか？	*Mado wo shimete itadakemasuka?*
Can you play the recording again, please?	もう一度録音を再生していただけますか？	*Mou ichido rokuon wo saisei shite itadakemasuka?*

English Phrase	Japanese	Transliteration
How do you pronounce that?	それはどうやって発音するの？	*Sore wa douyatte hatsuon suruno?*
My spellings are not great	私のスペリングは良くないです	*Watashi no superingu wa yokunai desu*
Why would you do that?	どうしてそんなことをしたの？	*Doushite sonna koto wo shitano?*
What Is the difference?	違いは何ですか？	*Chigai wa nandesuka?*
I would like to change my seat in class	席替えをしてもいいですか？	*Sekigae wo shitemo iidesuka?*
What makes you believe that?	どうしてそう思う？	*Doushite souomou?*
How often do you attend the library?	どれくらいの頻度で図書館に行きますか？	*Dorekurai no hindo de toshokan ni ikimasuka?*
You should silent study more often	もっとサイレントスタディをするべきです	*Motto sairento sutadi wo suru bekidesu*
How do you stay so focused?	どうやって集中力を維持していますか？	*Douyatte shuuchuuryoku wo iji shite imasuka?*
Did you oversleep?	寝坊した？	*Nebou shita?*
Could you come to the front of the class?	教室の前まで来ていただけますか？	*Kyoushitsu no mae made kite itadakemasuka?*
Who is next on the list?	次は誰ですか？	*Tsugi wa dare desuka?*
We'll have to stop the class there	そこで授業を止めるべきですね	*Sokode jugyou wo yameru bekidesune*
Hold on a moment	ちょっと待ってください	*Chotto matte kudasai*

Chapter 5: Vocabulary

Vocabulary	Japanese	Transliteration
Morning	朝	*asa*
Students	学生	*gakusei*
Register	登録	*touroku*
Begin	始める	*hajimeru*
Lesson	レッスン	*ressun*
Interrupt	割り込む	*warikomu*
Class	授業	*jugyou*
Seat	席	*seki*
Half-term	中間	*chuukan*
Break	休憩	*kyuukei*
Groups	グループ	*Guru-pu*
Answer	答え	*kotae*
Question	質問	*shitsumon*
Raise	上げる	*ageru*

Vocabulary	Japanese	Transliteration
Voice	*声*	*koe*
Read	*読む*	*yomu*
Activity	*活動*	*katsudou*
Finish	*完了*	*kanryou*
Blinds	*ブラインド*	*buraindo*
Attendance	*出席*	*shusseki*
Poor	*乏しい*	*toboshii*
Classroom	*教室*	*kyoushitsu*
Results	*結果*	*kekka*
Detention	*居残り*	*inokori*
Timetable	*時間割*	*jikanwari*
Textbook	*教科書*	*kyoukasho*
Mathematics	*数学*	*suugaku*
Science	*科学*	*kagaku*

Vocabulary	Japanese	Transliteration
English	*英語*	*eigo*
Favorite	*お気に入り*	*okiniiri*
Subject	*科目*	*kamoku*
Passed	*通過*	*tsuuka*
Failed	*失敗*	*shippai*
Exam	*試験*	*shiken*
Lunch break	*昼休憩*	*hirukyuukei*
Pencil	*鉛筆*	*empitsu*
Ruler	*定規*	*jougi*
Rubber	*消しゴム*	*keshigomu*
Concept	*概念*	*gainen*
Air conditioning	*エアコン*	*eakon*
Excuses	*言い訳*	*iiwake*
Nervous	*緊張*	*kinchou*

Vocabulary	Japanese	Transliteration
Distracted	*気が散る*	*kigachiru*
Friends	*友達*	*tomodachi*
Work ethic	*労働倫理*	*roudourinri*
Cafeteria	*カフェテリア*	*kafeteria*
Bell	*ベル*	*beru*
Graduation	*卒業*	*sotsugyou*
Ill	*病気*	*byouki*
Cancelled	*中止*	*chuushi*
University	*大学*	*daigaku*
Presentation	*プレゼンテーション*	*Purezente-shon*
Attention	*注目*	*chuumoku*
Compulsory	*義務*	*gimu*
Modules	*追加の*	*tsuikano*
Faculty	*学部*	*gakubu*

Vocabulary	Japanese	Transliteration
Entry requirements	*エントリー要件*	*Entori-youken*
Tuition fees	*授業料*	*jugyouryou*
Parents evening	*保護者会*	*hogoshakai*
Certificate	*証明書*	*shoumeisho*
Academic	*教師*	*kyoushi*
Accommodation	*宿泊施設*	*shukuhakushisetsu*
Part-time	*パートタイム*	*Pa-totaimu*
Full-time	*フルタイム*	*furutaimu*
Room mate	*ルームメイト*	*Ru-mumeito*
Deadline	*締切*	*shimekiri*
Self-funded	*自己資金*	*jikoshikin*
Loan	*ローン*	*Ro-n*
Workload	*仕事量*	*shigotoryou*
Scholarship	*奨学金*	*shougakukin*

Vocabulary	Japanese	Transliteration
Project	*プロジェクト*	*purojekuto*
Submitted	*提出済み*	*Teishutsu zumi*
Additional	*追加の*	*tsuikano*
Research	*調査*	*chousa*
Curriculum vitae	*履歴書*	*rirekisho*
Meeting	*会議*	*kaigi*
Supervisor	*上司*	*joushi*
Office	*オフィス*	*ofisu*
Support	*サポート*	*Sapo-to*
Improve	*改善する*	*kaizensuru*
Grade	*学年*	*gakunen*
Career	*キャリア*	*kyaria*
Plan	*計画*	*keikaku*
Field	*分野*	*Bun-ya*

Vocabulary	Japanese	Transliteration
Expertise	専門知識	Senmon chishiki
Qualified	認証済み	ninshouzumi
Enjoy	楽しむ	tanoshimu
Discussion	議論	giron
Member	メンバー	Menba-
Staff	スタッフ	sutaffu
Apprenticeship	アプレンティスシップ	Apurentisu shippu
Semester	学期	gakki
Trip	旅行	ryokou
Assignment	割り当て	wariate
Bursury	奨学金	shougakukin
Dormitory	寮	ryou
Curriculum	カリキュラム	karikyuramu
Memorize	覚える	oboeru

Vocabulary	Japanese	Transliteration
Notes	*注意書き*	*chuuigaki*
Recording	*録音*	*rokuon*
Pronounce	*発音*	*hatsuon*
Spelling	*スペリング*	*superingu*
Library	*図書室*	*toshositsu*
Focused	*集中する*	*shuuchuusuru*

Chapter 6: Marriage/Dating/Relationships

English Phrase	Japanese	Transliteration
Congratulations on your big day!	*おめでとう！*	*Omedetou!*
What time is the wedding?	*結婚式は何時ですか？*	*Kekkonshiki wa nanji desuka!*
I can't wait for your wedding!	*結婚式が待ちきれない！*	*Kekkonshiki ga machikirenai!*
Your wedding dress is beautiful	*美しいウエディングドレスですね*	*Utsukushii uedingu doresu desune*
Where did you get that ring from?	*指輪はどちらでご購入されたんですか？*	*Yubiwa wa dochira de gokounyuu saretandesuka?*
Where is the after party?	*二次会はどこで開催しますか？*	*Nijikai wa dokode kaisai shimasuka?*
Where are you going for your honeymoon?	*新婚旅行はどこにいくんですか？*	*Shinkon ryokou wa doko ni ikundesuka?*
I love your suit	*素敵なスーツですね*	*Suteki na su-tsu desune*
You guys look good together!	*二人ともお似合いですよ！*	*Futari tomo oniai desuyo!*
Thank you for the invitation	*ご招待ありがとう*	*Goshoutai arigatou*
I loved the food at your wedding	*結婚式のお食事はとても良かったです*	*Kekkonshiki no oshokuji wa totemo yokatta desu*
It was an emotional moment	*感動的な瞬間でした*	*Kandouteki na shunkan deshita*
May you live a happy married life!	*素敵な結婚生活を！*	*Suteki na kekkon seikatsu wo!*
I wish you the best for the future	*末永くお幸せに*	*Suenagaku oshiawase ni*

English Phrase	Japanese	Transliteration
I got engaged last week	*先週婚約しました*	*Senshuu kon-yaku shimashita*
I love you	*愛してる*	*aishiteru*
Let's go out later	*後で出かけよう*	*Atode dekakeyou*
Where should we go later?	*後でどこに行こうか？*	*Atode doko ni ikouka?*
Let's go shopping	*買い物に行こう*	*Kaimono ni ikou*
What's for dinner?	*晩ご飯は何？*	*Bangohan wa nani?*
I'll see you later	*またあとで*	*Mata atode*
I've missed you	*会いたかったです*	*Aitakatta desu*
Have you proposed already?	*プロポーズはもうした？*	*Puropo-zu wa mou shita?*
She got a divorce	*彼女は離婚した*	*Kanojo wa rikon shita*
I'm busy today	*今日は忙しいです*	*Kyou wa isogashii desu*
The bride and groom were kissing	*新郎新婦はキスしてた*	*Sinrou shinpu wa kisu shiteta*
The music at your wedding was great!	*結婚式での音楽はとても素敵でした！*	*Kekkonshiki deno ongaku wa totemo suteki deshita!*
When is the photographer arriving?	*写真家はいつ到着しますか？*	*Shashinka wa itsu touchaku shimasuka?*

English Phrase	Japanese	Transliteration
Thank you for the bouquet	*花束をありがとう*	*Hanataba wo arigatou*
You are so romantic!	*とてもロマンティックです！*	*Totemo romantikku desu!*
The gifts were lovely	*引き出物可愛かったです*	*Hikidemono kawaikatta desu*
Thank you so much!	*ありがとう！*	*Arigatou!*
I have always had a crush on you!	*ずっと好きでした！*	*Zutto suki deshita!*
The date was great	*素敵なデートでした*	*Suteki na de-to deshita*
A sense of humor is important	*ユーモアのセンスが大事だよ*	*Yu-moa no sensu ga daiji dayo*
You look gorgeous today	*今日はとってもゴージャスですね*	*Kyou wa tottemo go-jasu desune*
Thank you for being so considerate	*ご丁寧にありがとうございます*	*Goteinei ni arigatou gozaimasu*
Do you want to go to the cinema later?	*後で映画でも見に行く？*	*Atode eiga demo mini iku?*
Give me a kiss	*キスして*	*Kisu shite*
Give me a cuddle	*抱きしめて*	*dakishimete*
We have a lot in common	*私たちはたくさん共通点があるよ*	*Watashitachi wa takusan kyoutsuuten ga aruyo*
Today is our 5-year anniversary!	*今日は5年目の記念日！*	*Kyou wa gonenme no kinenbi!*

English Phrase	Japanese	Transliteration
What shall we do on valentine's day?	*バレンタインデーは何をしようか？*	*Barentainde- wa nani wo shiyouka?*
We'll get through it together	*一緒に乗り越えていきましょう*	*Issho ni norikoete ikimashou*
I'm sorry about that!	*ごめんなさい！*	*Gomen nasai!*
You know I'm always here for you!	*いつでも君のそばにいるよ*	*Itsudemo kimi no soba ni iruyo*
Can you advise me on that?	*アドバイスをもらえるかい？*	*Adobaisu wo moraeru kai?*
I really appreciate that	*本当に感謝しています*	*Hontou ni kansha shiteimasu*
That left me heartbroken	*がっかりだったよ*	*Gakkari dattayo*
I love your hair today	*今日の髪型は素敵だね*	*Kyou no kamigata wa suteki dane*
Your skin is glowing!	*お肌が輝いてるよ！*	*Ohada ga kagayaiteruyo!*
Can I buy you a drink?	*一杯奢らせてくれる？*	*Ippai ogorasete kureru?*
You are so attractive	*とても魅力的だね*	*Totemo miryokuteki dane*
Do you like me?	*私のこと好き？*	*Watashi no koto suki?*
What Is your phone number?	*電話番号は何番ですか？*	*Denwa bangou wa nanban desuka?*
I love your smile	*君の笑顔が大好きだ*	*Kimi no egao ga daisukida*

English Phrase	Japanese	Transliteration
Thank you for the compliments	お褒めにあずかり光栄です	*Ohome ni azukari kouei desu*
When can I meet your parents?	いつご両親にお会いできますか？	*Itsu goryoushin ni oai dekimasuka?*
I'd love to do that	そうしたいです	*Soushitai desu*
Would you like a dance?	踊りませんか？	*Odorimasenka?*
You are my type	あなたは私のタイプです	*Anata wa watashi no taipu desu*
I like the chemistry between us	私たち相性いいですね	*Watashi tachi aishou iidesune*
I like your vibe	あなたの雰囲気好きですよ	*Anata no fun-iki suki desuyo*
Stop flirting!	いちゃつかないで！	*Ichatsukanaide!*
I think we get along well	私たちよく気が合いますね	*Watashi tachi yoku ki ga aimasune*
We need to speak	話があります	*Hanashi ga arimasu*
I think we should break up	私たち別れた方が良いと思う	*Watashi tachi wakareta hou ga ii to omou*
You should dump him!	彼は捨てるべきよ！	*Kare wa suterubekiyo!*
I think that guy is a player!	あの人は遊び人だと思うよ！	*Ano hito wa asobinin dato omouyo!*
Does he really love you?	彼は本当にあなたを愛しているの？	*Kare wa hontou ni anata wo aishite iruno?*

English Phrase	Japanese	Transliteration
There's plenty of fish in the sea (Expression)	*相手なんて他にいくらでもいるよ*	*Aite nante hoka ni ikurademo iruyo*
Look at those lovebirds	*見てよあの素敵なカップル*	*Miteyo ano suteki na kappuru*
What's your type?	*どんな人がタイプ？*	*Donna hito ga taipu?*
I don't believe in love at first sight	*一目ぼれなんて信じない*	*Hitomebore nante shinjinai*
The love is real	*愛は本物です*	*Ai wa honmono desu*
I would never cheat on you!	*浮気なんて絶対しません！*	*Uwaki nante zettai shimasen*
Would you marry me?	*結婚してくれますか？*	*Kekkon shite kuremasuka?*
Let's go on a hike together	*一緒にハイキングに行こう*	*Issho ni haikingu ni ikou*
I am so over him!	*彼のことはもう吹っ切れたよ*	*Kare no koto wa mou fukkiretayo*
The situation is now awkward	*気まずい状況ですね*	*Kimazui joukyou desune*
I think we are compatible	*私たちはとても相性がいいと思う*	*Watashitachi wa totemo aishou ga ii to omou*
I don't see this working out	*上手くいくとは思いません*	*Umaku ikutowa omoimasen*
Where do you see yourself in 5 years?	*5年後どうしてると思う？*	*Gonengo doushiteru to omou?*
Where do you see yourself in 10 years?	*10年後どうしてると思う？*	*Juunengo doushiteru to omou?*

English Phrase	Japanese	Transliteration
I fell for him	彼に恋をした	Kare ni koi wo shita
I love your outfit	素敵な服ですね	Suteki na fuku desune
Can you wait for me in the car?	車で待っていてくれる？	Kuruma de matteite kureru?
Let's hang out more	もっと遊ぼうよ	Motto asobouyo
You mean everything to me!	あなたは私のすべてです！	Anata wa watashi no subete desu
I don't think I can live without you!	あなた無しでは生きていけない！	Anata nashidewa ikite ikenai!
You are my whole world	あなたは私の世界全てです	Anata wa watashi no sekai no subete desu
That was my first kiss	それが私のファーストキスでした	Sore ga watashi no fa-suto kisu deshita
I can't wait to meet your parents!	あなたのご両親とお会いするのが待ちきれない！	Anata no goryoushin to oai suru noga machikirenai!
I don't like that	それは嫌だ	Sore wa iya da
Don't say that!	そんなこと言わないで！	Sonnna koto iwanaide!
I met him online	彼とはオンラインで出会いました	Kare to wa onrain de deaimashita
I turned him down	私は彼を振りました	Watashi wa kare wo furimashita
We have a lot in common	私たち共通点がたくさんありますね	Watashitachi kyoutsuuten ga takusan arimasune

Chapter 6: Vocabulary

Vocabulary	Japanese	Transliteration
Wedding	結婚	*Kekkon*
Congratulations	おめでとう	*omedetou*
Wedding dress	ウエディングドレス	*Uedingu doresu*
Beautiful	美しい	*utsukushii*
Ring	指輪	*Yubiwa*
Party	パーティ	*Pa-ti*
Honeymoon	新婚旅行	*Shinkon ryokou*
Suit	スーツ	*Su-tsu*
Invitation	招待	*shoutai*
Emotional	感動的	*kandouteki*
Future	未来	*mirai*
Engaged	婚約した	*Kon-yaku shita*
Proposed	プロポーズした	*Puropo-zu shita*
Divorce	離婚	*rikon*

Vocabulary	Japanese	Transliteration
Busy	忙しい	*isogashii*
Bridge	橋	*hashi*
Groom	新郎	*shinrou*
Kiss	キス	*kisu*
Photographer	写真家	*shashinka*
Bouquet	花束	*hanataba*
Romance	ロマンス	*romansu*
Gift	贈り物	*okurimono*
Crush	壊れる	*kowareru*
Date	デート	*De-to*
Humor	ユーモア	*Yu-moa*
Gorgeous	ゴージャス	*Go-jasu*
Considerate	思いやりのある	*Omoiyari no aru*
Cinema	映画	*eiga*

Vocabulary	Japanese	Transliteration
Cuddle	*抱きしめる*	*dakishimeru*
Anniversary	*記念*	*kinen*
Valentine's day	*バレンタインデー*	*Barentainde-*
Heartbreak	*傷心*	*shoushin*
Skin	*肌*	*hada*
Glowing	*輝いている*	*kagayaiteiru*
Attractive	*魅力的*	*miryokuteki*
Smile	*笑顔*	*egao*
Compliment	*誉め言葉*	*Home kotoba*
Parents	*ご両親*	*goryoushin*
Dance	*ダンス*	*dansu*
Type	*タイプ*	*taipu*
Chemistry	*化学反応*	*Kagaku hannou*
Vibe	*雰囲気*	*Fun-iki*

Vocabulary	Japanese	Transliteration
Flirting	*いちゃつく*	*Ichatsuku*
Break up	*別れる*	*wakareru*
Dump	*捨てる*	*suteru*
Player	*遊び人*	*asobinin*
Fish	*魚*	*sakana*
Sea	*海*	*umi*
Lovebirds	*カップル*	*kappuru*
Cheat	*浮気*	*uwaki*
Marriage	*結婚*	*kekkon*
Hike	*ハイキング*	*haikingu*
Awkward	*気まずい*	*kimazui*
Compatible	*互換性*	*gokansei*
Outfit	*服*	*fuku*
Common	*一般的*	*ippanteki*

Chapter 7: Emotions & feelings

English Phrase	Japanese	Transliteration
I'm feeling happy	幸せです	*Shiawase desu*
I'm feeling sad	悲しいです	*Kanashii desu*
I'm feeling angry	怒っています	*okotteimasu*
I'm feeling disgusted	うんざりしています	*Unzari shiteimasu*
I'm feeling content	満たされています	*Mitasarete imasu*
I'm feeling peace	平穏を感じています	*Heion wo kanjite imasu*
I'm feeling excited	ワクワクしています	*Wakuwaku shiteimasu*
I'm feeling satisfied	満足しています	*Manzoku shiteimasu*
I'm feeling anguish	苦悩しています	*Kunou shiteimasu*
I'm feeling worried	心配しています	*Shimpai shiteimasu*
I'm feeling stressed	ストレスを感じています	*Sutoresu wo kanjite imasu*
I'm feeling anxious	不安です	*Fuan desu*
I'm feeling lost	喪失感があります	*Soushitsukan ga arimasu*
I'm feeling miserable	惨めです	*Mijime desu*

English Phrase	Japanese	Transliteration
I'm feeling confused	*混乱しています*	*Konran shiteimasu*
I'm feeling doubtful	*疑わしいです*	*Utagawashii desu*
I'm feeling desperate	*絶望的な気分です*	*Zetsubou teki na kibun desu*
I'm feeling mad	*怒っています*	*Okotte imasu*
I'm feeling insulted	*侮辱された気分です*	*Bujoku sareta kibun desu*
I'm feeling offended	*気分が悪いです*	*Kibun ga warui desu*
I'm feeling hopeless	*絶望的な気分です*	*Zetsubou teki na kibun desu*
I'm feeling grieved	*嘆かわしいです*	*Nagekawashii desu*
I'm feeling amused	*面白がっています*	*Omoshirogatte imasu*
I'm feeling prideful	*誇らしいです*	*Hokorashii desu*
I'm feeling lonely	*寂しいです*	*Sabishii desu*
I'm feeling frustrated	*いらいらしています*	*Iraira shite imasu*
I'm feeling vengeful	*復讐心に燃えています*	*Fukushuushin ni moete imasu*
I'm feeling depressed	*落ち込んでいます*	*Ochikonde imasu*

English Phrase	Japanese	Transliteration
I'm really excited about that!	*とても興奮しています！*	*Totemo koufun shiteimasu!*
Do you feel guilty about it?	*罪悪感はないの？*	*Zaiakukan wa naino?*
Hatred is not good!	*憎悪はよくない！*	*Zouo wa yokunai!*
Those people are jealous of you	*あなたに嫉妬してるんだよ*	*Anata ni shitto shiterundayo*
Jealousy is real	*嫉妬心は本物*	*Shittoshin wa honmono*
Why is she so arrogant?	*彼女はどうしてあんなに横柄なの？*	*Kanojo wa doushite annani ouhei nano?*
Don't be so lazy!	*だらだらしないで！*	*Daradara shinaide!*
I was anticipating that	*そう予想していましたよ*	*Sou yosou shite imashitayo*
Why are you so moody/?	*どうしてそんなに不機嫌なんですか？*	*Doushite sonnani fukigen nandesuka?*
Don't you think that is alarming?	*由々しき事態だと思いませんか？*	*Yuyushiki jitai dato omoimasenka?*
You don't want to annoy him!	*彼を困らせたくないんです！*	*Kare wo komarasetaku naindesu!*
Why do you isolate yourself from everyone?	*どうしてみんなから孤立しようとするの？*	*Doushite minna kara koritsu shiyouto suruno?*
Why are you so careless?	*どうしてそんなに注意不足なの？*	*Doushite sonnani chuui busoku nano?*
Why are you so reckless?	*どうしてそんなに乱暴なの？*	*Doushite sonnani ranbou nano?*

English Phrase	Japanese	Transliteration
That is astonishing to hear!	*聞いて驚きましたよ！*	*Kiite odorokimashitayo!*
Are you insecure?	*不安ですか？*	*Fuan desuka?*
That is nasty!	*最低です！*	*Saitei desu!*
I'm numb to the pain	*痛みに鈍感です*	*Itami ni donkan desu*
I love your optimism	*あなたの楽観的なところが好きです*	*Anata no rakkanteki na tokoro ga suki desu*
Why are you so pessimistic?	*どうしてそんなに悲観的になるの？*	*Doushite sonnani hikanteki ni naruno?*
Don't be cruel to animals	*動物に残酷なことをしないで*	*Doubutsu ni zankoku na koto wo shinaide*
I'm delighted to meet you!	*お会いできて嬉しいです！*	*Oai dekite ureshii desu*
We were in shock!	*私たちは衝撃を受けました！*	*Watashi tachi wa shougeki wo ukemashita!*
That is cowardly	*卑怯だな*	*Hikyou dana*
Always be polite to people	*常に礼儀正しくありなさい*	*Tsuneni reigi tadashiku arinasai*
That is not comfortable	*快適ではないですね*	*Kaiteki dewa nai desune*
You have to be patient	*辛抱しなきゃ*	*Shinbou shinakya*
You cheeky boy!	*生意気な少年！*	*Namaiki na shounen!*

English Phrase	Japanese	Transliteration
That's a pity!	お気の毒に！	*Okinodokuni!*
I am powerless	私は無力だ	*Watashi wa muryoku da*
I'm curious; that's all	ただ興味があった、それだけです	*Tada kyoumi ga atta, soredake desu*
I love your courage	あなたの勇気が大好きです	*Anata no yuuki ga daisuki desu*
I'm determined to make things right!	全てを正すと決めました！	*Subete wo tadasu to kimemashita!*
I regret doing that	それについて後悔しています	*Sore ni tsuite koukai shite imasu*
I dislike that person	あの人が嫌いです	*Ano hito ga kirai desu*
I was powerless in that situation	あの状況では私は無力だった	*Ano joukyou dewa watashi wa muryoku datta*
I'm pleased to announce that	発表できてうれしいです	*Happyou dekite ureshii desu*
That is so demoralizing	とてもがっかりですね	*Totemo gakkari desune*
Don't let that distract you	気を散らさないで	*Ki wo chirasanaide*
That is so ruthless	とても無慈悲ですね	*Totemo mujihi desune*
That was distressing to see	見ていて辛かったです	*Mite ite tsurakatta desu*
You have to face your fears!	恐怖に向き合いなさい！	*Kyoufu ni mukiai nasai!*

English Phrase	Japanese	Transliteration
Don't feel disheartened about it	*がっかりしないで*	*Gakkari shinaide*
I was reluctant to go with it	*同調するのは嫌だった*	*Douchou suru nowa iya datta*
The man was very polite	*その人はとても礼儀正しかったです*	*Sono hito wa totemo reigi tadashikatta desu*
That is so embarrassing!	*すごく恥ずかしい！*	*Sugoku hazukashii!*
I'm eager to get started	*是非始めたいです*	*Zehi hajimetai desu*
Don't be scared	*怖がらないで*	*Kowagaranaide*
Everything will be okay!	*全部上手くいくよ！*	*Zenbu umaku ikuyo!*
I loved your surprise earlier	*さっきのサプライズは素敵だったよ*	*Sakki no sapuraizu wa suteki datta yo*
You must have been suffering	*苦しんでいたに違いない*	*Kurushinde ita ni chigainai*
I am thankful for that	*それについては大変感謝しています*	*Sore ni tsuite wa taihen kansha shite imasu*
I don't trust him	*彼のことは信じない*	*Kare no koto wa shinjinai*
You are vulnerable	*傷つきやすいんですね*	*Kizutsukiyasuindesune*
Don't be impatient	*せっかちにならないで*	*Sekkachi ni naranaide*
I don't like the uncertainty	*頼りなくて好きになれない*	*Tayorinakute suki ni narenai*

English Phrase	Japanese	Transliteration
I felt the tension	*緊張した*	*Kinchou shita*
Don't tolerate that!	*許してはいけません！*	*Yurushitewa ikemasen!*
That made me very upset	*とても動揺させられた*	*Totemo douyou saserareta*
I don't mean to offend you	*あなたを怒らせるつもりはありません*	*Anata wo okoraseru tsumori wa arimasen*
I feel homesick	*ホームシックだ*	*Ho-mushikku da*
I'm unsure about that	*確信は持てない*	*Kakushin wa motenai*
Don't be so greedy!	*欲張らないで！*	*Yokubaranaide!*
I was horrified!	*ぞっとした！*	*Zottoshita!*
I hope you can turn it around	*立ち直ることを祈るよ*	*Tachinaoru koto wo inoruyo*
I sympathize with you	*同情するよ*	*Doujou suruyo*
I am so grateful for that	*とても感謝しています*	*Totemo kansha shiteimasu*
I feel sick today	*今日は具合が悪いです*	*Kyou wa guai ga warui desu*
I am energetic in the morning	*朝は元気です*	*Asa wa genki desu*
That moment was intense	*あの時はきつかったね*	*Ano toki wa kitsukatta ne*

English Phrase	Japanese	Transliteration
You are very lucky!	あなたはとても幸運だ！	*Anata wa totemo kouun da!*
I have been longing for that	それを切望してきた	*Sore wo setsubou shitekita*
I am very keen to get started	始める気満々です	*Hajimeru ki manman desu*
Don't irritate me!	イライラさせないで！	*Iraira sasenaide!*
Help out the needy	貧しい人たちを支援して	*Mazushii hitotachi wo shien shite*
I am passionate about that	それに情熱を注いでいます	*Sore ni jounetsu wo sosoide imasu*
That is very powerful	それはとても強力だ	*Sore wa totemo kyouryoku da*
That is sensitive information	それは機密情報です	*Sore wa kimitsu jouhou desu*
I am shocked by the outcome!	結果に衝撃を受けました！	*Kekka ni shougeki wo ukemashita!*
You left me speechless!	呆れて何も言えない！	*Akirete nani mo ienai!*
Don't humiliate me!	侮辱しないで！	*Bujoku shinaide!*
I have a lot of admiration for you	すごく感心してるよ	*Sugoku kanshin shiteruyo*
I did not anticipate that	それは見越していなかった	*Sore wa mikoshite inakatta*
Do not become attached	執着しないで	*Shuuchaku shinaide*

English Phrase	Japanese	Transliteration
Show some compassion	*共感してよ*	*Kyoukan shiteyo*
I am low on confidence	*自信がありません*	*Jishin ga arimasen*
You are very courageous	*とても勇敢ですね*	*Totemo yuukan desune*
I am craving that	*それを渇望している*	*Sore wo katsubou shiteiru*
I am feeling disappointed	*がっかりだよ*	*Gakkari dayo*
Don't feel discouraged	*自信を無くさないで*	*Jishin wo nakusanaide*
I am devoted to my work	*自分の仕事に専念しています*	*Jibun no shigoto ni sennen shite imasu*
I doubt that is true	*真実かどうか疑わしい*	*Shinjitsu ka douka utagawashii*
I dread that day	*その日が怖いよ*	*Sono hi ga kowaiyo*
You are a humble person	*謙虚な人ですね*	*Kenkyo na hito desune*
I am feeling the nostalgia!	*懐かしいね！*	*Natsukashiine!*
Don't panic!	*落ち着いて！*	*Ochitsuite!*
I am feeling remorseful	*後悔している*	*Koukai shiteiru*
I am not worried about that	*それについては心配していないよ*	*Sore ni tsuite wa shinpai shite inai yo*

English Phrase	Japanese	Transliteration
It was lovely seeing you earlier	*お会いできてよかったです！*	*Oai dekite yokatta desu!*
Are you satisfied with that?	*ご満足いただけましたか？*	*Gomanzoku itadakemashitaka?*
It is important for me	*それは私にとって重要です*	*Sore wa watashi ni totte juuyou desu*
You are a strong man!	*強い人ですね！*	*Tsuyoi hito desune!*
That is well-built!	*頑丈ですね！*	*Ganjou desune!*
I am not fond of that	*それは好きじゃない*	*Sore wa suki janai*
You are hot-tempered	*短気ですね*	*Tanki desune*
I feel provoked	*刺激的だ*	*Shigekiteki da*
That's the spirit! (expression)	*その調子！*	*Sono choushi!*
That is appalling of you!	*最悪だな！*	*Saiaku danal*
Don't violate the rules!	*ルールを破るな！*	*Ru-ru wo yaburuna!*
Why do you doubt yourself?	*なぜ自分自身を疑う？*	*Naze jibun jishin wo utagau?*
I'm unsure about that	*確証は持てません*	*Kakushou wa motemasen*
Stop being so indecisive!	*ぐずぐずするな！*	*Guzuguzu suruna!*

English Phrase	Japanese	Transliteration
You are very stubborn!	*頑固ですね！*	*Ganko desune!*
I am interested in that	*興味があります*	*Kyoumi ga arimasu*
I'm hungry	*お腹がすいた*	*Onaka ga suita*
I'm thirsty	*喉が渇いた*	*Nodo ga kawaita*
You are stupid!	*バカ！*	*Baka!*
He is an envious person	*彼がうらやましいよ*	*Kare ga urayamashii yo*
I am ecstatic for you!	*あなたに夢中です！*	*Anata ni muchuu desu!*
I am so proud of you!	*あなたを誇りに思います！*	*Anata wo hokori ni omoimasu!*
You hurt me!	*あなたは私を傷つけた！*	*Anata wa watashi wo kizu tsuketa!*
He was very smug	*彼は独善的だった*	*Kare wa dokuzendeki datta*
I was very skeptical	*私はとても懐疑的だった*	*Watashi wa totemo kaigiteki datta*
I'm starving!	*とてもお腹がすいています！*	*Totemo onaka ga suite imasu!*
Why are you surprised?	*どうして驚いたの？*	*Doushite odoroitano?*
You have to be confident	*自信を持たなくちゃ*	*Jishin wo motanakucha*

English Phrase	Japanese	Transliteration
That really irritated me!	マジでイライラする！	*Maji de iraira suru!*
I am intrigued!	興味をそそられます！	*Kyoumi wo sosoraremasu!*
I am overwhelmed with work	作品に圧倒されています	*Sakuhin ni attou sareteimasu*
I am over the moon! (expression)	嬉しくてたまらないよ！	*Ureshikute tamaranaiyo!*
I was reluctant to do it	気が進まなかった	*Ki ga susumanakatta*
Why are you so tense?	どうしてそんなに緊張しているの？	*Doushite sonnani kinchou shite iruno?*
That's wonderful news!	素晴らしいニュースだ！	*Subarashii nyu-su da!*
I feel cheated!	騙された気分だ！	*Damasareta kibun da!*
That's disappointing to hear!	聞いてがっかりしたよ！	*Kiite gakkari shitayo!*
I'm feeling emotional!	感動的だ！	*Kandouteki da!*
You are innocent	あなたは無実だ	*Anata wa mujitsu da*
Why are you so aggressive?	どうしてそんなに攻撃的なの？	*Doushite sonnani kougekiteki nano?*
That's very strange	とても変ですね	*Totemo hen desune*
I'm very upset	困ったな	*komattana*

English Phrase	Japanese	Transliteration
I like your enthusiasm	*あなたの熱意が好きだ*	*Anata no netsui ga suki da*
Are you self-dependent?	*自立していますか？*	*Jiritsu shite imasuka?*
Are you scared?	*怖いの？*	*Kowai no?*
Are you afraid of rejection?	*嫌われるのが怖いの？*	*Kirawareru no ga kowaino?*
I love your passion!	*あなたの情熱が好きです！*	*Anata no jounetsu ga suki desu!*
You are self-assured	*自信家ですね！*	*Jishinka desune!*
I am dying of rage! (Expression)	*死ぬほど腹が立つ！*	*Shinu hodo haraga tatsu!*
Could you imagine the outrage?	*その暴虐を想像できますか？*	*Sono bougyaku wo souzou dekimasuka?*
That's naughty	*やんちゃですね*	*Yancha desune*
I'm an outgoing person	*私は外交的です*	*Watashi wa gaikouteki desu*
Why are you so grumpy?	*どうしてそんなに不機嫌なんですか？*	*Doushite sonnani fukigen nandesuka?*
That is very disturbing	*とても不安ですね*	*Totemo fuan desune*
I'm introverted	*私は内向的です*	*Watashi wa naikouteki desu*
I'm extroverted	*私は外交的です*	*Watashi wa gaikouteki desu*

English Phrase	Japanese	Transliteration
I'm feeling the agony	苦しいです	*Kurushii desu*
You don't have to suffer in silence	黙って苦しむ必要はありません	*Damatte kurushimu hitsuyou wa arimasen*
You are very fortunate	とても幸運ですね	*Totemo kouun desune*
I'm feeling energetic	元気いっぱいです	*Genki ippai desu*
You are clever	賢いですね	*Kashikoi desune*
I feel at ease	楽になりました	*Raku ni narimashita*
Don't act impulsively!	衝動的にならないで！	*Shoudouteki ni naranaide!*
I love the devotion	献身的な姿勢がすばらしいです	*Kenshinteki na shisei ga subarashii desu*
Don't be so nosy!	お節介はやめて！	*Osekkai wa yamete!*
That touched me	感動しました	*Kandou shimashita*
Your child is rebellious!	あなたの子供は反抗的ですね！	*Anata no kodomo wa hankouteki desune!*
I'm hopeful that things will change	状況が変わることを祈ります	*Joukyou ga kawaru koto wo inorimasu*
Are you able to do that?	これできる？	*Kore dekiru?*
You are incapable	役に立ちませんね	*Yaku ni tachimasen ne*

Chapter 7: Vocabulary

Vocabulary	Japanese	Transliteration
Happy	幸せ	*Shiawase*
Sad	悲しみ	*Kanashimi*
Angry	怒り	*ikari*
Disgusted	うんざり	*unzari*
Content	コンテンツ	*kontentsu*
Peace	平和	*heiwa*
Excited	興奮した	*Koufun shita*
Satisfied	満足した	*Manzoku shita*
Anguish	苦悩	*kunou*
Worried	心配した	*Shinpai shita*
Stressed	緊張した	*Kinchou shita*
Anxious	気になる	*kininaru*
Miserable	惨め	*mijime*
Confused	混乱した	*Konran shita*

Vocabulary	Japanese	Transliteration
Doubtful	疑わしい	*utagawashii*
Desperate	自暴自棄	*jiboujiki*
Mad	怒った	*Okotta*
Insulted	侮辱された	*Bujoku sareta*
Offended	気分を害した	*Kibun wo gaishita*
Hopeless	絶望的	*Zetsubou teki*
Grieved	悲しんだ	*kanashinda*
Amused	面白がる	*omoshirogaru*
Prideful	誇り高い	*hokoritakai*
Lonely	寂しい	*sabishii*
Frustrated	欲求不満	*yokkyuufuman*
Vengeful	復讐心	*fukushuushin*
Depressed	おちこんでいる	*Ochikonde iru*
Guilty	罪悪感を感じる	*Zaiakukan wo kanjiru*

Vocabulary	Japanese	Transliteration
Hatred	悲しみ	*kanashimi*
Jealous	嫉妬	*shitto*
Arrogant	傲慢	*gouman*
Lazy	怠惰	*taida*
Moody	不機嫌な	*Fukigen na*
Alarming	驚くべき	*odorokubeki*
Isolate	隔離する	*Kakuri suru*
Careless	不注意	*fuchuui*
Reckless	乱暴	*ranbou*
Astonishing	驚くべき	*Odoroku beki*
Insecure	不安	*Fuan*
Nasty	汚らわしい	*kegarawashii*
Pain	痛み	*itami*
Optimistic	楽観的	*Rakkan teki*

Vocabulary	Japanese	Transliteration
Pessimistic	*悲観的*	*Hikan teki*
Cruel	*残酷*	*zankoku*
Delighted	*幸せ*	*shiawase*
Shock	*衝撃*	*shougeki*
Coward	*臆病者*	*Okubyou mono*
Polite	*丁寧*	*teinei*
Comfortable	*快適*	*kaiteki*
Patient	*忍耐強い*	*Nintai zuyoi*
Cheeky	*生意気*	*namaiki*
Pity	*残念*	*Zan-nen*
Powerless	*無力*	*muryoku*
Curious	*興味深い*	*Kyoumi bukai*
Courage	*勇気*	*yuuki*
Determined	*断固とした*	*Danko toshita*

Vocabulary	Japanese	Transliteration
Regret	後悔	*koukai*
Dislike	嫌い	*kirai*
Pleased	喜んで	*yorokonde*
Demoralizing	意気消沈	*Iki shouchin*
Ruthless	無慈悲	*mujihi*
Distressing	悲惨な	*Hisan na*
Disheartened	がっかり	*gakkari*
Reluctant	気が進まない	*Ki ga susumanai*
Polite	丁寧	*Teinei*
Embarrassing	恥ずかしい	*hazukashii*
Eager	熱心な	*Nesshin na*
Scared	怖い	*Kowai*
Suffering	苦しむ	*kurushimu*
Thankful	感謝している	*Kansha shiteiru*

Vocabulary	Japanese	Transliteration
Trust	信じる	shinjiru
Vulnerable	傷つきやすい	Kizutsuki yasui
Impatient	せっかち	sekkachi
Uncertain	不確か	futashika
Tension	テンション	tenshon
Tolerate	許容する	Kyoyou suru
Upset	動揺	douyou
Offend	怒らせる	okoraseru
homesick	ホームシック	Ho-mushikku
Greedy	欲張りな	Yokubarina
Horrified	恐ろしい	osoroshii
Sympathy	共感	kyoukan
Grateful	ありがたい	arigatai
Energetic	元気いっぱいな	Genki ippai na

Vocabulary	Japanese	Transliteration
Luck	幸運	*kouun*
Keen	鋭い	*surudoi*
Irritate	いらいらする	*Iraira suru*
Needy	貧しい	*mazushii*
Passionate	情熱的な	*Jounetsu teki na*
Powerful	力強い	*Chikarazuyoi*
Sensitive	繊細な	*Sensai na*
Shocked	衝撃を受けた	*Shougeki wo uketa*
Speechless	何も言えない	*Nani mo ienai*
Humiliate	屈辱を与える	*Kutsujoku wo ataeru*
Admiration	感心	*Kanshin*
Anticipation	期待	*kitai*
Attached	優しい	*yasashii*
Compassion	同情	*doujou*

Vocabulary	Japanese	Transliteration
Confidence	自信	*jishin*
Courageous	勇気のある	*Yuuki no aru*
Craving	切望する	*Setsubou suru*
Disappointed	失望した	*Shitsubou shita*
Discouraged	がっかりした	*Gakkari shita*
Devoted	献身的	*Kenshin teki*
Humble	謙虚	*kenkyo*
Nostalgia	懐かしさ	*natsukashisa*
Panic	慌てる	*awateru*
Remorse	悔いる	*kuiru*
Worried	心配する	*Shinpai suru*
Important	重要	*juuyou*
Hot tempered	短気	*tanki*
Provoked	じらされた	*jirasareta*

Vocabulary	Japanese	Transliteration
Appalling	ぞっとする	*Zotto suru*
Violate	違反する	*Ihan suru*
Indecisive	ぐずぐずする	*Guzuguzu suru*
Stubborn	頑固	*ganko*
Interested	興味がある	*Kyoumi ga aru*
Hungry	空腹	*kuufuku*
Thirsty	喉が渇いた	*Nodo ga kawaita*
Stupid	バカ	*baka*
Envious	うらやましい	*urayamashii*
Ecstatic	夢中	*muchuu*
Proud	誇る	*hokoru*
Skeptical	懐疑的	*Kaigi teki*
Starving	飢えている	*ueteiru*
Surprised	驚いた	*odoroita*

Vocabulary	Japanese	Transliteration
Confident	*自信がある*	*Jishin ga aru*
Irritated	*イライラする*	*Iraira suru*
Intrigued	*興味をそそる*	*Kyoumi wo sosoru*
Overwhelmed	*圧倒された*	*Attou sareta*
Reluctant	*気が進まない*	*Ki ga susumanai*
Tense	*緊迫した*	*Kinpaku shita*
Cheat	*騙す*	*damasu*
Disappointing	*がっかり*	*gakkari*
Emotional	*感情的*	*Kanjou teki*
Innocent	*無垢な*	*Muku na*
Aggressive	*攻撃的*	*Kougeki teki*
Upset	*動揺*	*douyou*
Enthusiasm	*熱意*	*netsui*
Self-dependent	*自立した*	*Jiritsu shita*

Vocabulary	Japanese	Transliteration
Self-assured	物怖じしない	*Monooji shinai*
Outrage	怒り	*ikari*
Naughty	やんちゃ	*yancha*
Grumpy	不機嫌	*fukigen*
Disturbing	不穏な	*Fuon na*
Introvert	内向的	*naikouteki*
Extrovert	外交的	*gaikouteki*
Agony	苦痛	*kutsuu*
Fortunate	幸運な	*Kouun na*
Energetic	元気いっぱいの	*Genki ippai no*
Clever	賢い	*Kashikoi*
Impulsive	衝動的	*Shoudou teki*
Devote	献身	*kenshin*
Nosy	お節介な	*Osekkai na*
Rebellious	反抗的	*Hankou teki*
Incapable	無能	*munou*

Chapter 8: Sports & Hobbies

English Phrase	Japanese	Transliteration
Do you plan any sports?	*スポーツの予定はありますか？*	*Supo-tsu no yotei wa arimasuka?*
Do you watch soccer?	*サッカーは見ますか？*	*Sakka- wa mimasuka?*
Did you see the game last night?	*昨夜の試合は観ましたか？*	*Sakuya no shiai wa mimashitaka?*
The league is very competitive	*リーグはとても競争が激しい*	*Ri-gu wa totemo kyousou ga hageshii*
Did you see the boxing?	*ボクシングは観ましたか？*	*Bokushingu wa mimashitaka?*
That game was so fun!	*あの試合はとても楽しかった！*	*Ano shiai wa totemo tanoshikatta!*
Are you coming to practice this week?	*今週は練習に来ますか？*	*Konshuu wa renshuu ni kimasuka?*
I look forward to the game	*試合が楽しみです*	*Shiai ga tanoshimi desu*
How often do you exercise?	*どれくらいの頻度で運動しますか？*	*Dorekurai no hindo de undou shimasuka?*
I like to go out for a jog	*ジョギングが好きです*	*Jogingu ga suki desu*
I like that player	*あの選手が好きです*	*Ano senshu ga suki desu*
I like that team	*あのチームが好きです*	*Ano chi-mu ga sukidesu*
I love basketball	*バスケットボールが大好きです*	*Basuketto bo-ru ga daisuki desu*
I love tennis	*テニスが大好きです*	*Tenisu ga daisuki desu*

English Phrase	Japanese	Transliteration
I love hockey	ホッケーが大好きです	*Hokke- ga daisuki desu*
I love the atmosphere	あの雰囲気が好きです	*Ano fun-iki ga suki desu*
Do you practice regularly?	定期的に練習しますか？	*Teikiteki ni renshuu shimasuka?*
You're late for training!	トレーニングに遅刻しています！	*Tore-ningu ni chikoku shite imasu!*
Do you have the correct footwear?	正しい靴を履いていますか？	*Tadashii kutsu wo haite imasuka?*
The coach threw in the towel	コーチがタオルを投げた	*Ko-chi ga taoru wo nageta*
That team lost	あのチームは負けた	*Ano chi-mu wa maketa*
Don't sweat it! (Expression)	心配するな！	*Shinpai suruna!*
This is a long match	長い試合だ	*Nagai shiai da*
Are you going to the game later?	後で試合に行きますか？	*Ato de shiai ni ikimasuka?*
Give it your best shot	思いっきりやってみて	*Omoikkiri yatte mite*
The game went the distance	試合はやり切った	*Shiai wa yarikitta*
The team set the pace for the game	あのチームが試合の主導権を握った	*Ano chi-mu ga shiai no shudouken wo nigitta*
The game is in the final stages	試合は最終局面だ	*Shiai wa saishuu kyokumen da*

English Phrase	Japanese	Transliteration
The game went down to the wire (expression)	*試合は最後まで接戦でした*	*Shiai wa saigo made sessen deshita*
The arena was packed out	*アリーナは満席でした*	*Ari-na wa manseki deshita*
How do athletes live like that?	*アスリートはどうやってそんな風に生きるんだ？*	*Asuri-to wa douyatte sonna fuuni ikirunda?*
The awards ceremony started	*表彰式が始まりました*	*Hyoushoushiki ga hajimarimashita*
He captained the team	*彼はそのチームのキャプテンを務めた*	*Kare wa sono chi-mu no kyaputen wo tsutometa*
You are the champion!	*あなたがチャンピオンです！*	*Anata ga chanpion desu!*
The fans cheered the team on	*ファンはチームを応援した*	*Fan wa chi-mu wo ouen shita*
The coach watched on the sideline	*コーチは傍観していた*	*Ko-chi wa boukan shiteita*
Are you competing this year?	*今年は参戦しますか？*	*Kotoshi wa sansen shimasuka?*
The competition is fierce	*その対戦は苛烈だ*	*Sono taisen wa karetsu da*
The team was defeated	*そのチームは負けた*	*Sono chi-mu wa maketa*
I will defend my team until the end	*私は最後までチームを守る*	*Watashi wa saigo made chi-mu wo mamoru*
What was the final score?	*最終結果はどうでしたか？*	*Saishuu kekka wa dou deshita ka?*
Are you into fitness?	*フィットネスに興味はありますか？*	*Fittonesu ni kyoumi wa arimasuka?*

English Phrase	Japanese	Transliteration
The players took a break at half-time	*選手たちはハーフタイムで休憩をとった*	*Senshu tachi wa ha-futaimu de kyuukei wo totta*
The judges were biased	*審判が偏った判断をしていた*	*Shinpan ga katayotta handan wo shiteita*
Which league do you play in?	*どのリーグでプレイしますか？*	*Dono ri-gu de purei shimasuka?*
The opponent was tough	*相手は強かった*	*Aite ha tsuyokatta*
You had a great performance	*良いパフォーマンスをしていますね*	*Ii pafo-mansu wo shite imasune*
You are in great shape	*引き締まった体をしていますね*	*Hikishimatta karada wo shite imasune*
I love your physique	*良い体格をしていますね*	*Ii taikaku wo shite imasune*
Are you a team player?	*あなたはチームプレイヤーですか？*	*Anata wa chi-mu pureiya- desuka*
You have to follow the rules of the game	*試合のルールに従ってください*	*Shiai no ru-ru ni shitagatte kudasai*
The player missed the shot	*その選手はシュートを外した*	*Sono senshu wa shu-to wo hazushita*
That was great sportsmanship	*素晴らしいスポーツマンシップでした*	*Subarashii supo-tsuman shippu deshita*
That was a hard tackle	*きついタックルでしたね*	*Kitsui takkuru deshita ne*
The tactics were unclear	*戦術が不透明でしたね*	*Senjutsu ga futoumei deshita ne*
You are very talented	*とても才能がありますね*	*Totemo sainou ga arimasu ne*

English Phrase	Japanese	Transliteration
That was great teamwork!	素晴らしいチームワークでした！	*Subarashii chi-muwa-ku deshita!*
The game was a tie!	試合は引き分けでした！	*Shiai wa hikiwake deshita!*
When is the tournament?	トーナメントはいつですか？	*To-namento wa itsu desuka?*
The referee blew his whistle	審判は笛を吹いた	*Shinpan wa fue wo fuita*
The spectators were loud	観客は大声でした	*Kankyaku wa oogoe deshita*
The tactics were ineffective	その戦術は効果がありませんでした	*Sono senjutsu wa kouka ga arimasen deshita*
The team was winning	そのチームが勝っていた	*Sono chi-mu ga katteita*
The team was losing	そのチームが負けていた	*Sono chi-mu ga maketeita*
What are your hobbies?	ご趣味はなんですか？	*Goshumi wa nandesuka?*
I like traveling	旅行が好きです	*Ryokou ga suki desu*
I like cooking	料理が好きです	*Ryouri ga suki desu*
I like reading books	読書が好きです	*Dokusho ga suki desu*
Do you do the gardening?	ガーデニングはしますか？	*Ga-deningu wa shimasuka?*
How often do you play computer games?	ゲームはどれくらいしますか？	*Ge-mu wa dorekurai shimasuka?*

English Phrase	Japanese	Transliteration
What do you do in your free time?	*暇な時は何をしますか？*	*Hima na toki wa nani wo shimasuka?*
I love listening to music	*音楽を聴くのが好きです*	*Ongaku wo kiku noga suki desu*
You are a great dancer	*あなたは素晴らしいダンサーです*	*Anata wa subarashii dansa- desu*
What interests you?	*何に興味がありますか？*	*Nani ni kyoumi ga arimasuka?*
I am into comics	*漫画に夢中です*	*Manga ni muchuu desu*
How often do you do it?	*どれくらいの頻度でそれをしますか？*	*Dorekurai no hindo de sore wo shimasuka?*
Where do you do it?	*どこでしますか？*	*Dokode shimasuka?*
I like outdoor activities	*アウトドア好きです*	*Autodoa zuki desu*
I'm an amateur footballer	*サッカーのアマチュア選手です*	*Sakka- no amachua senshu desu*
I want to travel the world	*世界を旅行したい*	*Sekai wo ryokou shitai*
Did you join them?	*それに参加しましたか？*	*Sore ni sanka shimashitaka?*
I signed up for a gym membership	*ジムに会員登録をした*	*Jimu ni kaiin touroku wo shita*
He didn't turn up	*彼は現れませんでした*	*Kare wa arawaremasen deshita*
I like to stay at home	*家にいるのが好きです*	*Ie ni iru no ga suki desu*

Chapter 8: Vocabulary

Vocabulary	Japanese	Transliteration
Sports	スポーツ	*Supo-tsu*
Soccer	サッカー	*Sakka-*
Game	試合	*shiai*
League	リーグ	*Ri-gu*
Competitive	競争が激しい	*Kyousou ga hageshii*
Boxing	ボクシング	*bokushingu*
Practice	練習	*renshuu*
Exercise	エクササイズ	*ekusasaizu*
Jog	ジョギング	*jogingu*
Team	チーム	*Chi-mu*
Basketball	バスケットボール	*Basuketto bo-ru*
Tennis	テニス	*tenisu*
Atmosphere	雰囲気	*Fun-iki*
Hockey	ホッケー	*Hokke-*

Vocabulary	Japanese	Transliteration
Training	*トレーニング*	*Tore-ningu*
Footwear	*履物*	*Hakimono*
Coach	*コーチ*	*Ko-chi*
Distance	*距離*	*kyori*
Arena	*アリーナ*	*Ari-na*
Athlete	*アスリート*	*Asuri-to*
Award	*賞*	*shou*
Ceremony	*式典*	*shikiten*
Captain	*キャプテン*	*kyaputen*
Champion	*チャンピオン*	*chanpion*
Cheer	*応援*	*ouen*
Sideline	*サイドライン*	*saidorain*
Compete	*競争*	*kyousou*
Fierce	*激しい*	*hageshii*

Vocabulary	Japanese	Transliteration
Defeat	*敗北*	*haiboku*
Defend	*守る*	*mamoru*
Score	*点数*	*tensuu*
Fitness	*フィットネス*	*fittonesu*
Break	*休憩*	*kyuukei*
Judges	*審判*	*shinpan*
Bias	*偏った*	*katayotta*
League	*リーグ*	*Ri-gu*
Opponent	*相手*	*aite*
Tough	*強い*	*tsuyoi*
Performance	*パフォーマンス*	*Pafo-mansu*
Physique	*体格*	*taikaku*
Rules	*ルール*	*Ru-ru*
Missed	*ミス*	*misu*

Vocabulary	Japanese	Transliteration
Sportsmanship	*スポーツマンシップ*	*Supo-tsuman shippu*
Tackle	*タックル*	*takkuru*
Tackle	*タックル*	*takkuru*
Tactics	*戦術*	*senjutsu*
Unclear	*不透明*	*futoumei*
Talent	*才能がある*	*Sainou ga aru*
Teamwork	*チームワーク*	*Chi-muwa-ku*
Tie	*同点*	*douten*
Tournament	*トーナメント*	*To-namento*
Referee	*レフェリー*	*Referi-*
Whistle	*笛*	*fue*
Spectators	*観客*	*kankyaku*
Ineffective	*効果がない*	*Kouka ga nai*
Winning	*勝利*	*shouri*

Vocabulary	Japanese	Transliteration
Losing	敗北	*haiboku*
Hobbies	趣味	*shumi*
Traveling	旅行	*ryokou*
Cooking	料理	*ryouri*
Reading	読む	*yomu*
Gardening	ガーデニング	*Ga-deningu*
Computer	コンピュータ	*Konpyu-ta*
Music	音楽	*ongaku*
Dance	ダンス	*dansu*
Interests	興味	*Kyoumi*
Comics	漫画	*manga*
Outdoor activities	野外活動	*Yagai katsudou*
Amateur footballer	アマチュアサッカー選手	*Amachua sakka- senshu*
Gym membership	ジムのメンバーシップ	*Jimu no menba- shippu*

Chapter 9: Accessories

English Phrase	Japanese	Transliteration
I like your watch!	*素敵な時計ですね！*	*Suteki na tokei desune!*
Bring an umbrella	*傘を持ってきて*	*Kasa wo mottekite*
I like your necklace!	*素敵なネックレスですね！*	*Suteki nanekkuresu desune!*
I left my purse at home	*財布を家に忘れてきました*	*Saifu wo ie ni wasurete kimashita*
Did you wash your socks?	*靴下は洗いましたか？*	*Kutsushita wa araimashitaka?*
Please wear an apron	*エプロンを着てください*	*Epuron wo kite kudasai*
Do you have any jewelry?	*ジュエリーは持っていますか？*	*Jueri- wa motte imasuka?*
Where did you get your handbag from?	*そのハンドバッグはどこで手に入れましたか？*	*Sono handobaggu wa doko de teni iremashitaka?*
The wardrobe is full	*ワードローブがいっぱいです*	*Wa-doro-bu ga ippai desu*
It is well made	*よくできていますね*	*Yoku dekite imasune*
This is a vintage item	*これはビンテージ品です*	*Kore wa binte-ji hin desu*
This is my wedding ring	*これは私の結婚指輪です*	*Kore wa watashi no kekkon yubiwa desu*
I am old-fashioned	*私は時代遅れです*	*Watashi wa jidai okure desu*
This is a luxury item	*これは高級品です*	*Kore wa koukyuu hin desu*

English Phrase	Japanese	Transliteration
The fabric is good	良い生地ですね	*Ii kiji desu ne*
This is cheap	これは安いです	*Kore wa yasui desu*
This is expensive	これは高いです	*Kore wa takai desu*
I love these sunglasses	良いサングラスですね	*Ii sangurasu desu ne*
I don't like your taste	あなたの嗜好は好きじゃない	*Anata no shikou wa suki janai*
That's my preference	それが私の好みです	*Sore ga watashi no konomi desu*
That is my stylist	私のスタイリストです	*Watashi no sutairisuto desu*
A helmet is important	ヘルメットは大事です	*Herumetto wa daiji desu*
The luggage was overweight	荷物が重すぎました	*Nimotsu ga omosugi mashita*
That is a lovely scarf	素敵なスカーフですね	*Suteki na suka-fu desune*
Those shoes are stylish	スタイリッシュな靴ですね	*Sutairisshu na kutsu desune*
Your buttons are undone	ボタンを閉め忘れていますよ	*Botan wo shime wasurete imasuyo*
Can you bring some tissue paper?	ティッシュペーパーを持ってきてくれる？	*Tisshu pe-pa- wo motte kite kureru?*
This is made from cotton	これは綿でできています	*Kore wa wata de dekite imasu*

English Phrase	Japanese	Transliteration
This is made from polyester	*これはポリエステル製です*	*Kore wa poriesuteru sei desu*
This is made from wool	*これは羊毛製です*	*Kore wa youmou sei desu*
This is made from silk	*これはシルク製です*	*Kore wa shiruku sei desu*
This is made from nylon	*これはナイロン製です*	*Kore wa nairon sei desu*
Bikinis are forbidden here	*ここではビキニは禁止です*	*Koko dewa bikini wa kinshi desu*
Where is your jumper from?	*そのジャンパーはどこで手に入れましたか？*	*Sono janpa- wa dokode teni iremashitaka?*
Here are your flip flops	*これがあなたのサンダルです*	*Kore ga anata no sandaru desu*
What is your uniform?	*あなたの制服は何ですか？*	*Anata no seifuku ha nandesuka?*
I love your blazer	*良いブレザーですね*	*Ii bureza- desune*
What do you wear to work?	*何を着て仕事をしますか？*	*Nani wo kite shigoto wo shimasuka?*
Can you give me the clippers?	*爪切りを貸していただけますか？*	*Tsumekiri wo kashite itadakemasuka?*
I love your socks	*いい靴下ですね*	*Ii kutsushita desune*
I love that scent	*素敵な香水ですね*	*Suteki na kousui desune*
Where is your cologne from?	*そのコロンはどこで手に入れましたか？*	*Sono koron wa doko de te ni iremashitaka?*

Chapter 9: Vocabulary

Vocabulary	Japanese	Transliteration
Watch	*腕時計*	*Udedokei*
Umbrella	*傘*	*kasa*
Necklace	*ネックレス*	*nekkuresu*
Purse	*財布*	*saifu*
Socks	*靴下*	*kutsushita*
Apron	*エプロン*	*epuron*
Jewelry	*ジュエリー*	*Jueri-*
Handbag	*ハンドバッグ*	*handobaggu*
Wardrobe	*ワードローブ*	*Wa-doro-bu*
Vintage	*ビンテージ*	*Binte-ji*
Fashion	*ファッション*	*fasshon*
Luxury	*高級な*	*Koukyuu na*
Fabric	*生地*	*kiji*
Cheap	*安い*	*yasui*

Vocabulary	Japanese	Transliteration
Expensive	高い	*takai*
Sunglasses	サングラス	*sangurasu*
Taste	味	*aji*
Preference	好み	*konomi*
Style	スタイル	*sutairu*
Helmet	ヘルメット	*herumetto*
Luggage	荷物	*nimotsu*
Scarf	スカーフ	*Suka-fu*
Button	ボタン	*botan*
Tissue paper	ティッシュペーパー	*Tisshupe-pa-*
Cotton	綿	*wata*
Polyester	ポリエステル	*poriesuteru*
Wool	羊毛	*youmou*
Silk	シルク	*shiruku*

Vocabulary	Japanese	Transliteration
Nylon	*ナイロン*	*nairon*
Bikini	*ビキニ*	*bikini*
Forbidden	*禁止*	*kinshi*
Jumper	*ジャンパー*	*Janpa-*
Flip flops	*サンダル*	*sandaru*
Uniform	*制服*	*seifuku*
Blazer	*ブレザー*	*Bureza-*
Clippers	*爪切り*	*tsumekiri*
Scent	*香水*	*kousui*
Cologne	*コロン*	*koron*

Chapter 10: Asking & Giving Directions

English Phrase	Japanese	Transliteration
Excuse me, could you help?	すみません、手伝っていただけませんか？	*Sumimasen, tesudatte itadakemasenka?*
Do you know how I can get to..	どうすれば...に辿り着けますか？	*Dousureba ... ni tadoritsuke masuka?*
How far is that from here?	そこまではどれくらいかかりますか？	*Sokomade wa dorekurai kakari masuka?*
Can you tell me if I am going the right way?	この道で合ってますか？	*Kono michi de atte masuka?*
Is there a shorter route?	もっと近い道はありますか？	*Motto chikai michi wa arimasuka?*
What is the best way to..	最善の道のりはどれですか？	*Saizen no michinori wa dore desuka?*
Follow the road ahead	道なりに進んでください	*Michinari ni susunde kudasai*
Go straight ahead	まっすぐ進んでください	*Massugu susunde kudasai*
It's around the corner	角を曲がったあたりです	*Kado wo magatta atari desu*
Cross the road ahead	道の向こうです	*Michi no mukou desu*
The next road after the roundabout	回り道の次の道	*Mawari michi no tsugi no michi*
Are there any shops around here?	このあたりにお店はありますか？	*Kono atari ni omise wa arimasuka?*
Where can I find the bank?	銀行はどこですか？	*Ginkou wa doko desuka?*
Take the next right	次を右折してください	*Tsugi wo usetsu shite kudasai*

English Phrase	Japanese	Transliteration
Take the next left	次を左折してください	Tsugi wo sasetsu shite kudasai
It's a short ride ahead	車ですぐですよ	Kuruma de sugu desuyo
There is a quicker route	もっと早いルートがありますよ	Motto hayai ru-to ga arimasuyo
That is the wrong direction	こっちは違う方向ですよ	Kocchi wa chigau houkou desuyo
It's half a mile from here	ここから半マイルです	Koko kara han mairu desu
It's a mile from here	ここから1マイルです	Koko kara ichi mairu desu
It's a five-minute walk from here	ここから徒歩五分です	Koko kara toho gofun desu
It's a ten-minute walk from here	ここから徒歩十分です	Koko kara toho juppun desu
Opposite this road	道の反対側	Michi no hantai gawa
Can you show me the map?	地図を見せていただけますか？	Chizu wo misete itadakemasuka?
I think there is construction on this road	この道は工事中だと思います	Kono michi wa koujichuu dato omoimasu
Is there parking there?	そこに駐車場はありますか？	Soko ni chuushajou wa arimsau ka?
There's no parking	駐車場はありません	Chuushajou wa arimasen
Sorry, I wouldn't know	すみません、知りません	Sumimasen, shirimasen

English Phrase	Japanese	Transliteration
I'm not from around here	私はこのあたりの出身ではありません	*Watashi wa kono atari no shusshin dewa arimasen*
There is a busy road ahead	この先は混んでいます	*Kono saki wa konde imasu*
There is a junction ahead	この先に交差点があります	*Kono saki ni kousaten ga arimasu*
Ask that man over there	あちらの男性に聞いてください	*Achira no dansei ni kiite kudasai*
Let me show you	お見せします	*Omise shimasu*
Pardon me; I'm lost	すみません、道に迷いました	*Sumimasen, michi ni mayoi mashita*
Make a left turn	左折してください	*Sasetsu shite kudasai*
Make a right turn	右折してください	*Usetsu shite kudasai*
Where is the supermarket	スーパーマーケットはどこですか	*Su-pa-ma-ketto wa doko desuka*
It's not too far from here	そんなに遠くないですよ	*Sonnani tooku naidesuyo*
It is within walking distance from here?	ここから徒歩圏内ですか？	*Kokokara toho kennnai desuka?*
It is within driving distance from here?	ここから車で行ける距離ですか？	*Koko kara kuruma de ikeru kyori desuka?*
How far is the hospital from here?	ここから病院までどれくらいですか？	*Koko kara byouin made dorekurai desuka?*
How far is the supermarket from here?	ここからスーパーマーケットまでどれくらいですか？	*Koko kara su-pa- ma-ketto made dorekurai desuka?*

English Phrase	Japanese	Transliteration
The traffic lights are red	信号は赤です	*Shingou wa aka desu*
The tunnel is ahead	トンネルはこの先です	*Tonneru wa kono saki desu*
That is a lit road	あちらの道は明るいです	*Achira no michi wa akarui desu*
Where is the metro station?	地下鉄の駅はどこですか？	*Chikatetsu no eki wa doko desuka?*
Take the second right	二つ目の角を右折してください	*Futatsume no kado wo usetsu shite kudasai*
Take the second left	二つ目の角を左折してください	*Futatsume no kado wo sasetsu shite kudasai*
There is a quicker way to get there	もっと早い道がありますよ	*Motto hayai michi ga arimasu yo*
Go up the hill	丘を登ってください	*Oka wo nobotte kudasai*
Go down the hill	丘を下ってください	*Oka wo kudatte kudasai*
Opposite the shops	お店の反対側	*Omise no hantai gawa*
Are there hotels nearby?	近くにホテルはありますか？	*Chikaku ni hoteru wa arimasuka?*
I'm looking for an ATM machine	ATMを探しています	*e-ti-emu wo sagashite imasu*
It's 100 meters ahead	100メートル先です	*Hyaku me-toru saki desu*
You won't be able to miss it	見逃すことはないと思います	*Minogasu koto wa nai to omoimasu*

English Phrase	Japanese	Transliteration
There is a sign ahead	*この先に看板があります*	*Kono saki ni kanban ga arimasu*
Continue on this road	*この道を進んでください*	*Kono michi wo susunde kudasai*
Got it!	*了解！*	*Ryoukai!*
Can you give me some directions?	*道順を教えていただけますか？*	*Michijun wo oshiete itadake masuka?*
Where is the nearest grocery store from here?	*一番近い食料品店はどこですか？*	*Ichiban chikai shokuryouhinten wa doko desuka?*
Can you guide me there?	*案内していただけますか？*	*Annai shite itadakemasuka?*
I'm looking for the town center	*街の中心を探しています*	*Machi no chuushin wo sagashite imasu*
The airport is ahead	*空港はこの先です*	*Kuukou wa kono saki desu*
Don't make a U-turn on this road	*この道でUターンしないでください*	*Kono michi de yu-ta-n shinaide kudasai*
That's not right	*違います*	*chigaimasu*
Watch out for the pedestrians	*歩行者にご注意ください*	*Hokousha ni gochuui kudasai*
It's around the corner from here	*ここからすぐ近くですよ*	*Kokokara sugu chikaku desuyo*
It's not too far from here	*ここからそう遠くないです*	*Koko kara sou tooku nai desuyo*
Follow the slip road	*出入道路に従ってください*	*Deiridouro ni shitagatte kudasai*

English Phrase	Japanese	Transliteration
It's Infront of you	*目の前にありますよ*	*Meno mae ni arimasuyo*
It's behind this building	*この建物の裏にあります*	*Kono tatemono no ura ni arimasu*
Follow the zebra crossing	*横断歩道に従ってください*	*Oudan hodou ni shitagatte kudasai*
There are crossroads ahead	*この先交差点があります*	*Kono saki kousaten ga arimasu*
Where does this road lead to?	*この道はどこに続いていますか？*	*Kono michi wa doko ni tsuzuite imasuka?*
Watch out for emerging traffic	*新しい渋滞に注意してください*	*Atarashii juutai ni chuui shite kudasai*
I'm sorry for bothering you	*お手数おかけして申し訳ありません*	*Otesuu okakeshite moushiwake arimasen*
I'm new here	*ここに来たばかりです*	*Koko ni kita bakari desu*
The first thing you'll see is..	*最初に見えるのは... です*	*Saisho ni mieru nowa... desu*
Stop right there	*そこで止まってください*	*Soko de tomatte kudasai*
It's really hard to miss	*見逃すことはないでしょう*	*Minogasu koto wa nai deshou*
Can you repeat those directions?	*もう一度教えていただけますか？*	*Mou ichido oshiete itadakemasuka?*
This route is quicker	*こちらの道が早いですよ*	*Kochira no michi ga hayai desuyo*
Could I ask for a favor?	*お願いしてもいいですか？*	*Onegai shitemo ii desuka?*

Chapter 10: Vocabulary

Vocabulary	Japanese	Transliteration
Shorter	より短い	Yori mijikai
Route	ルート	Ru-to
Ahead	先	Saki
Corner	角	kado
Cross	交差点	kousaten
Roundabout	回り道	mawarimichi
Quicker	より速い	Yori hayai
Wrong	間違い	machigai
Direction	方向	houkou
Mile	マイル	mairu
Walk	歩く	aruku
Opposite	反対側	hantaigawa
Map	地図	chizu
Construction	工事	kouji

Vocabulary	Japanese	Transliteration
Parking	*駐車場*	*chuushajou*
Junction	*交差点*	*kousaten*
Supermarket	*スーパーマーケット*	*Su-pa-ma-ketto*
Hospital	*病院*	*byouin*
Traffic Lights	*信号*	*shingou*
Lit road	*明るい道*	*Akarui michi*
Metro station	*地下鉄の駅*	*Chikatetsu no eki*
Hill	*丘*	*oka*
ATM machine	*ATM*	*e-ti-emu*
Sign	*看板*	*kanban*
Directions	*方向*	*houkou*
Grocery	*食料品*	*shokuryouhin*
Town Center	*中心街*	*chuushingai*
U-turn	*Uターン*	*Yu-ta-n*

Vocabulary	Japanese	Transliteration
Pedestrians	*歩行者*	*hokousha*
Corner	*角*	*kado*
Slip road	*出入道路*	*Deiri douro*
Infront	*前*	*mae*
Behind	*後ろ*	*ushiro*
Zebra crossing	*横断歩道*	*oudanhodou*
Crossroad	*交差点*	*kousaten*
Emerging traffic	*新しい渋滞*	*Atarashii juutai*
Route	*ルート*	*Ru-to*
Favor	*お願い*	*onegai*
Building	*建物*	*tatemono*

Chapter 11: Health & Fitness

English Phrase	Japanese	Transliteration
How often do you work out?	*どれくらいの頻度で運動しますか？*	*Dorekuraino hindo de undou shimasuka?*
Let's do the warm-up	*ウォームアップしましょう*	*Wo-muappu shimashou*
Let's do the warm-down	*ウォームダウンしましょう*	*Wo-mudaun shimashou*
Let's cooldown	*クールダウンしましょう*	*Ku-rudaun shimashou*
What's your diet like?	*食生活はどんな感じですか？*	*Shokuseikatsu wa donna kanji desuka?*
I am a vegan	*私はヴィーガンです*	*Watashi wa vi-gan desu*
I am a vegetarian	*私はベジタリアンです*	*Watashi wa bejitarian desu*
I follow a keto diet	*ケトジェニックダイエットをしています*	*Ketojenikku daietto wo shite imasu*
I follow a low-carb diet	*糖質制限ダイエットをしています*	*Toushitesu seigen daietto wo shite imasu*
I do intermittent fasting	*断続的に断食をしています*	*Danzokuteki ni danjiki wo shite imasu*
I follow a gluten-free diet	*グルテンフリーダイエットをしています*	*Gurutenfuri- daietto wo shite imasu*
That's my gym instructor	*あれは私のジムインストラクターだ*	*Are wa watashi no jimu insutorakuta- da*
I love yoga	*ヨガが大好きです*	*Yoga ga suki desu*
I exercise in the morning	*朝に運動します*	*Asa ni undou shimasu*

English Phrase	Japanese	Transliteration
I exercise in the afternoon	午後に運動します	Gogo ni undou shimasu
I exercise in the evening	夜に運動します	Yoru ni undou shimasu
Cut that out	切り落としてください	Kiriotoshite kudasai
Do you have a nuts allergy?	ナッツアレルギーはありますか？	Nattsu arerugi- wa arimasuka?
These ingredients are natural	これらの成分は天然のものです	Korera no seibun wa tennen no mono desu
Watch out for the bacteria	バクテリアに注意してください	Bakuteria ni chuui shite kudasai
This is not good for you	あなたにとって良くないよ	Anata ni totte yokunaiyo
What are the benefits?	利点は何ですか？	Riten wa nandesuka?
What is your blood pressure?	血圧を教えていただけますか？	Ketsuatsu wo oshiete itadakemasuka?
My body is sore	体が痛いです	Karada ga itai desu
I'm in a calorie deficit	カロリー不足です	Karori- busoku desu
I'm in a calorie surplus	カロリー過剰です	Karori- kajou desu
He suffered cardiac arrest	彼は心停止を起こした	Kare wa shinteishi wo okoshita
That's quite a challenge!	すごい挑戦ですね！	Sugoi chousen desune!

English Phrase	Japanese	Transliteration
What do you have for breakfast?	*朝食は何を食べますか？*	*Choushoku wa nani wo tabemasuka?*
What do you have for lunch?	*昼食は何を食べますか？*	*Chuushoku wa nani wo tabemasuka?*
What do you have for dinner?	*夕食は何を食べますか？*	*Yuushoku wa nani wo tabemasuka?*
Try to eat clean	*綺麗に食べてください*	*Kirei ni tabete kudasai*
Did you change your diet?	*食事を変えましたか？*	*Shokuji wo kaemashitaka?*
He collapsed on the track	*彼はトラックで倒れた*	*Kare wa torakku de taoreta*
I'm committed to my health	*健康管理に専念しています*	*Kenkou kanri ni sennen shite imasu*
I have bad conditioning	*調子が悪い*	*Choushi ga warui*
I have good conditioning	*調子がいい*	*Choushi ga ii*
You have poor stamina	*スタミナがないですね*	*Sutamina ga naidesune*
How do you cope with that?	*どう対処するんですか？*	*Dou taisho surundesuka?*
That's my favorite cuisine	*私のお気に入りの料理です*	*Watashi no okiniiri no ryouri desu*
I'm a bad cook	*私は料理が下手です*	*Watashi wa ryouri ga heta desu*
Is there a cure for this?	*これに対する治療法はありますか？*	*Kore ni taisuru chiryouhou ha arimasuka?*

English Phrase	Japanese	Transliteration
He has diabetes	*彼は糖尿病です*	*Kare wa tounyoubyou desu*
I feel dehydrated	*脱水症状です*	*Dassui shoujou desu*
I've never heard of that disease	*そんな病気は聞いたことがありません*	*Sonna byouki wa kiitakoto ga arimasen*
What dish are you cooking today?	*今日はどんな料理を作っているんですか？*	*Kyou wa donna ryouri wo tsukutte irundesuka?*
You have to stay disciplined	*規則を守らなきゃ*	*Kisoku wo mamoranakya*
Have you visited a doctor?	*お医者さんにかかったことはありますか？*	*Oishasan ni kakatta koto wa arimasuka?*
Have you visited a clinic?	*クリニックに行ったことはありますか？*	*Kurinikku ni itta koto wa arimasuka?*
Have you visited a therapist?	*セラピストに診てもらったことはありますか？*	*Serapisuto ni mite moratta koto wa arimasuka?*
Avoid alcohol at all costs	*アルコールは絶対に避けてください*	*Aruko-ru wa zettai ni sakete kudasai*
Is that drug legal?	*その薬は合法ですか？*	*Sono kusuri wa gouhou desuka?*
It has a positive effect	*良い効果があります*	*Ii kouka ga arimasu*
I am full of energy in the morning	*朝は元気いっぱいです*	*Asa wa genki ippai desu*
Be careful with that equipment	*その装置には気を付けてください*	*Sono souchi ni wa ki wo tsukete kudasai*
Don't throw away any excess	*余計なものを捨てないでください*	*Yokei na mono wo sutenaide kudasai*

English Phrase	Japanese	Transliteration
That was a good learning curve	*良い学習曲線でした*	*Ii gakushuu kyokusen deshita*
That was a good experience	*良い経験でした*	*Ii keiken deshita*
There are a few factors	*要因はいくつかあります*	*Youin wa ikutsuka arimasu*
I like to stay fit	*健康を管理するのが好きです*	*Kenkou wo kanri suru no ga suki desu*
Did you break it?	*壊したんですか？*	*Kowashitandesuka?*
Did you fracture it?	*骨折したんですか？*	*Kossetsu shitandesuka?*
You have great genetics	*良い遺伝子を持っていますね*	*Ii idenshi wo motte imasune*
What is your goal?	*目標は何ですか？*	*Mokuhyou wa nandesuka?*
You have grown so much	*良く成長しましたね*	*Yoku seichou shimashitane*
I need to stop these habits	*この習慣はやめなくちゃ*	*Kono shuukan wa yamenakucha*
That's harmful	*有害です*	*Yuugai desu*
That's healthy	*健康的です*	*Kenkouteki desu*
That's unhealthy	*不健康です*	*Fukenkou desu*
Where did you get those herbs?	*そのハーブはどこで手に入れましたか？*	*Sono ha-bu wa doko de te ni iremashitaka?*

English Phrase	Japanese	Transliteration
I only eat homemade food	*家庭料理しか食べません*	*Katei ryouri shika tabemasen*
Stop eating out so frequently!	*外食ばかりするのはやめなさい！*	*Gaishoku bakari suru no wa yamenasai!*
You are hygienic	*衛生的ですね*	*Eiseiteki desune*
You are unhygienic	*不衛生ですね*	*Fueisei desune*
I'm immune to that	*それに対しては免疫があります*	*Sore ni taishite wa men-eki ga arimasu*
You've improved a lot	*たくさん改善しましたね*	*Takusan kaizen shimashitane*
Watch out for the flue	*煙道に注意してください*	*Endou ni chuui shite kudasai*
Watch out for the virus	*ウイルスに注意してください*	*Uirusu ni chuui shite kudasai*
I have an infection	*感染症にかかっています*	*Kansenshou ni kakatte imasu*
You lack iron	*鉄分不足ですね*	*Tetsubun busoku desune*
That's pure laziness!	*それは純粋な怠惰です！*	*Sore wa junsui na taida desu!*
You need to change your lifestyle	*生活習慣を変えなくてはいけません*	*Seikatsu shuukan wo kaenakutewa ikemasen*
I don't take any medication	*薬は一つも使っていません*	*Kusuri wa hitotsumo tsukatte imasen*
Good memories, right?	*良い思い出ですね*	*Ii omoide desune*

English Phrase	Japanese	Transliteration
What's your metabolic rate?	*あなたの代謝率は？*	*Anata no taisharitsu wa?*
Minimize it as much as possible	*できるだけ小さくしてください*	*Dekirudake chiisaku shite kudasai*
It's a mixture of both	*両方の混合物です*	*Ryouhou no kongoubutsu desu*
Don't forget to stretch out!	*ストレッチを忘れずに！*	*Sutorecchi wo wasurezuni!*
Avoid nicotine	*ニコチンは避けてください*	*Nikochin wa sakete kudasai*
That is very nutritious	*とても栄養価が高いです*	*Totemo eiyouka ga takai desu*
Obesity is a big problem here	*肥満は大問題です*	*Himan wa daimondai desu*
That's an obstacle	*それは邪魔ですね*	*Sore wa jama desune*
I don't mean to be offensive	*攻撃的になるつもりはありません*	*Kougekiteki ni naru tsumori wa arimasen*
What a great opportunity!	*とてもいい機会だ！*	*Totemo ii kikaida!*
I'm optimistic about it	*それについては楽観的です*	*Sore ni tsuite wa rakkanteki desu*
I'm currently overweight	*太りすぎています*	*Futori sugitc imasu*
Why did you not participate?	*どうして参加しなかったんですか？*	*Doushite sanka shinakattandesuka?*
Keep track of my performance	*自分のパフォーマンスを追跡する*	*Jibun no pafo-mansu wo tsuiseki suru*

English Phrase	Japanese	Transliteration
That pharmacy might have it	*あの薬局ならあるかもしれませんよ*	*Ano yakkyoku nara aru kamo shiremasen yo*
I like to eat in small portions	*少しずつ食べるのが好きです*	*Sukoshizutsu taberu noga suki desu*
Be cautious; it is potent!	*気を付けて、効果が強いです！*	*Kiwo tsukete, kouka ga tsuyoi desu!*
Prevention is better than cure (expression)	*予防は治療に勝る*	*Yobou wa chiryou ni masaru*
That's promising	*頼もしいですね*	*Tanomoshii desune*
Protect yourself at all times	*常に自衛しなさい*	*Tsuneni jiei shinasai*
Looks like a puncture	*刺し傷みたいですね*	*Sashikizu mitai desune*
I'm currently in rehabilitation	*リハビリ中です*	*Rihabiri chuu desu*
Today is my day off	*今日は休みです*	*Kyou wa yasumi desu*
You have to be resilient!	*打たれ強くならなきゃ！*	*Utare zuyoku naranakya!*
That's your responsibility	*それはあなたの責任です*	*Sore wa anata no sekinin desu*
Is there any risk involved?	*リスクはありますか？*	*Risuku wa arimasuka?*
What's your role in all of this?	*これらにおけるあなたの役割は何ですか？*	*Korera ni okeru anata no yakuwari wa nandesuka?*
Don't rush!	*急がないで！*	*Isoganaide!*

English Phrase	Japanese	Transliteration
I'm allergic	*アレルギーがあります*	*Arerugi- ga arimasu*
What would you do in such a scenario?	*そんなシナリオで何をするつもり?*	*Sonna shinario de nani wo suru tsumori?*
Have you seen the scoreboard?	*結果表を見ましたか?*	*Kekkahyou wo mimashitaka?*
That's my specialty	*それが私の専門です*	*Sore ga watashi no senmon desu*
Don't add any spices	*調味料は一切入れないでください*	*Choumiryou wa issai irenaide kudasai*
That's the spirit!	*その調子!*	*Sono choushi!*
We are on a winning streak!	*連勝中です!*	*Renshouchuu desu!*
That requires a lot of strength	*大きな強さが必要です*	*Ookina tsuyosa ga hitsuyou desu*
It's normal to struggle	*苦戦するのは当たり前です*	*Kusen suru no wa atarimae desu*
We need your support!	*あなたの助けが必要です!*	*Anatano tasuke ga hitsuyou desu!*
Do you do any weight training?	*ウェイトトレーニングはしますか?*	*Ueito tore-ningu wa shimasuka?*
Do you do any cardio?	*有酸素運動はしますか?*	*Yuusanso undou wa shimasuka?*
I have the symptoms!	*症状が出ました!*	*Shoujou ga demashita!*
He kept taunting me!	*彼は私を罵倒し続けた!*	*Kare wa watashi wo batou shituzuketa!*

English Phrase	Japanese	Transliteration
It's very tempting!	*とても魅力的です！*	*Totemo miryokuteki desu!*
That is very therapeutic!	*とても癒されます！*	*Totemo iyasaremasu!*
I pulled a muscle	*肉離れを起こしました*	*Nikubanare wo okoshimashita*
What a great transformation	*すごい変化ですね！*	*Sugoi henka desune!*
Have you seen the latest trend?	*最近のトレンドは見ていますか？*	*Saikin no torendo wa mite imasuka?*
I hate vegetables	*野菜が嫌いです*	*Yasai ga kirai desu*
I love fruits	*フルーツが大好きです*	*Furu-tsu ga daisuki desu*
Victory is ours! (Expression)	*我々の勝利だ！*	*Wareware no shouri da!*
That is a violation of the rules!	*ルール違反です！*	*Ru-ru ihan desu!*
I did it voluntarily	*自主的にやりました*	*Jishuteki ni yarimashita*
He is vulnerable	*彼は傷つきやすい*	*Kare wa kizutsuki yasui*
I haven't explored that yet	*まだ調べていません*	*Mada shirabete imasen*
Did you take your medication?	*お薬は飲みましたか？*	*Okusuri wa nomimashitaka?*
It's your time to shine! (Expression)	*あなたが輝く時ですよ！*	*Anata ga kagayaku toki desuyo!*

English Phrase	Japanese	Transliteration
That is contagious	それは伝染します	*Sore wa densen shimasu*
That was really painful!	すごく痛かったです！	*Sugoku itakatta desu!*
Did you go in for a checkup?	検診には行きましたか？	*Kenshin niwa ikimashitaka?*
The injury worsened	怪我が悪化した	*Kega ga akka shita*
The injury got better	怪我が良くなった	*Kega ga yokunatta*
I'm currently in recovery	回復中です	*Kaifukuchuu desu*
Is there an alternative?	代替手段はありますか？	*Daitai shudan wa arimasuka?*
He was stuck in a coma	彼は昏睡していた	*Kare wa konsui shiteita*
Relax for a while	しばらく安静にしていてください	*Shibaraku ansei ni shiteite kudasai*
Is it curable?	これは治りますか？	*Kore wa naorimasuka?*
It's a chronic illness	慢性疾患です	*Mansei shikkan desu*
You have a calcium deficiency	カルシウム不足ですね	*Karushiumu busoku desune*
I think I am malnourished	栄養失調だと思います	*Eiyou shicchou dato omoimasu*
You have some good qualities	いくつか良い資質をお持ちですね	*Ikutsuka ii shishitsu wo omochi desune*

English Phrase	Japanese	Transliteration
Are you going in for treatment?	*治療しに行きますか？*	*Chiryou shini ikimasuka?*
You need to cut out the junk	*ジャンクフードは控える必要があります*	*Jankufu-do wa hikaeru hitsuyou ga arimasu*
I have lost my appetite	*食欲をなくしました*	*Shokuyoku wo nakushimashita*
Look at those biceps!	*見てよあの上腕二頭筋！*	*Miteyo ano jouwan nitoukin!*
I love your courage	*いい度胸だ*	*Ii dokyou da*
Have you seen a doctor?	*病院には行った？*	*Byouin niwa itta?*
I fractured my bone	*骨を折りました*	*Hone wo orimashita*
That is harmful	*有害です*	*Yuugai desu*
The area has inflammation	*ここが炎症を起こしていますね*	*Koko ga enshou wo okoshite imasune*
Do you have insurance?	*保険には入っていますか？*	*Hoken niwa haitte imasuka?*
The intensity is really high!	*強度はかなり高いです！*	*Kyoudo wa kanari takai desu!*
Have you seen the longevity?	*あのご長寿の方を見たことはありますか？*	*Ano gochouju no kata wo mitakotowa arimasuka?*
Remove the moisture	*水分を取り除く*	*Suibun wo torinozoku*
The game finished	*ゲームは終了しました*	*Ge-mu wa shuuryou shimashita*

Chapter 11: Vocabulary

Vocabulary	Japanese	Transliteration
Workout	運動	*undou*
Warm-up	ウォームアップ	*Wo-mu appu*
Warm-down	ウォームダウン	*Wo-mu daun*
Cooldown	クールダウン	*Ku-ru daun*
Diet	ダイエット	*Daietto*
Vegan	ヴィーガン	*vi-gan*
Vegetarian	ベジタリアン	*bejitarian*
Keto diet	ケトジェニックダイエット	*Ketojenikku daietto*
Low carb diet	糖質制限ダイエット	*Toushitsu seigen daietto*
Intermittent fasting	断続的な断食	*Danzokuteki na danjiki*
Gluten-free diet	グルテンフリーダイエット	*Guruten furi- daietto*
Instructor	インストラクター	*Insutorakuta-*
Yoga	ヨガ	*yoga*
Morning	朝	*asa*

Vocabulary	Japanese	Transliteration
Afternoon	*午後*	*gogo*
Evening	*夜*	*yoru*
Nuts	*ナッツ*	*nattsu*
Allergy	*アレルギー*	*Arerugi-*
Ingredients	*材料*	*zairyou*
Natural	*自然の*	*Shizen no*
Bacteria	*最近*	*saikin*
Benefits	*利点*	*riten*
Blood pressure	*血圧*	*ketsuatsu*
Sore	*痛み*	*itami*
Calories	*カロリー*	*Karori-*
Deficit	*欠乏*	*ketsubou*
Surplus	*余剰*	*yojou*
Cardiac arrest	*心停止*	*shinteishi*

Vocabulary	Japanese	Transliteration
Breakfast	*朝食*	*choushoku*
Lunch	*昼食*	*chuushoku*
Dinner	*夕食*	*yuushoku*
Collapse	*崩れる*	*kuzureru*
Track	*トラック*	*torakku*
Committed	*関与した*	*Kan-yo shita*
Health	*健康*	*kenkou*
Conditioning	*調節*	*chousetsu*
Stamina	*スタミナ*	*sutamina*
Cuisine	*料理*	*ryouri*
Cure	*治療*	*chiryou*
Diabetes	*糖尿病*	*tounyoubyou*
Dehydrated	*脱水*	*dassui*
Disease	*疾患*	*shikkan*

Vocabulary	Japanese	Transliteration
Discipline	*起立*	*kiritsu*
Doctor	*医者*	*isha*
Clinic	*クリニック*	*kurinikku*
Therapist	*セラピスト*	*serapisuto*
Alcohol	*アルコール*	*Aruko-ru*
Drug	*薬*	*kusuri*
Legal	*合法*	*gouhou*
Effect	*効果*	*kouka*
Energy	*エネルギー*	*Enerugi-*
Equipment	*装置*	*souchi*
Excess	*過剰*	*kajou*
Experience	*経験*	*keiken*
Fit	*合う*	*au*
Fracture	*骨折*	*kossetsu*

Vocabulary	Japanese	Transliteration
Genetics	遺伝学	*idengaku*
Goal	ゴール	*Go-ru*
Habit	習慣	*shuukan*
Harmful	害する	*gaisuru*
Herb	ハーブ	*Ha-bu*
Homemade	自家製	*jikasei*
Hygiene	衛生的	*eiseiteki*
Unhygienic	不衛生	*fueisei*
Immune	免疫	*Men-eki*
Flue	煙道	*endou*
Virus	ウイルス	*uirusu*
Infection	感染	*kansen*
Iron	鉄	*tetsu*
Lifestyle	ライフスタイル	*raifusutairu*

Vocabulary	Japanese	Transliteration
Medication	投薬	*touyaku*
Memory	記憶	*kioku*
Metabolic rate	代謝率	*taisharitsu*
Stretch	ストレッチ	*sutorecchi*
Nicotine	ニコチン	*nikochin*
Nutrition	栄養	*eiyou*
Obesity	肥満	*himan*
Obstacle	障害	*shougai*
Offensive	攻撃的	*kougekiteki*
Opportunity	機会	*kikai*
Underweight	低体重	*teitaijuu*
Overweight	太りすぎ	*futorisugi*
Pharmacy	薬局	*yakkyoku*
Portion	部分	*bubun*

Vocabulary	Japanese	Transliteration
Caution	注意	*chuui*
Prevention	予防	*yobou*
Cure	治す	*naosu*
Puncture	刺傷	*sashikizu*
Rehabilitation	リハビリテーション	*Rihabirite-shon*
Resilient	弾力のある	*Danryoku no aru*
Risk	危険	*kiken*
Allergy	アレルギー	*Arerugi-*
Scenario	シナリオ	*shinario*
Scoreboard	スコアボード	*Sukoabo-do*
Spice	スパイス	*supaisu*
Spirit	精神	*seishin*
Streak	連続	*renzoku*
Cardio	有酸素運動	*Yuusanso undou*

Vocabulary	Japanese	Transliteration
Symptom	*症状*	*shoujou*
Therapy	*治療*	*chiryou*
Muscle	*筋肉*	*kinniku*
Transformation	*変身*	*henshin*
Trend	*トレンド*	*torendo*
Vegetables	*野菜*	*yasai*
Fruits	*果物*	*kudamono*
Victory	*勝利*	*shouri*
Violation	*違反*	*ihan*
Voluntary	*自発的*	*jihatsuteki*
Vulnerable	*脆弱*	*zeijaku*
Contagious	*伝染性の*	*densenseino*
Checkup	*調べる*	*shiraberu*
Injury	*怪我*	*kega*

Vocabulary	Japanese	Transliteration
Recovery	*回復*	*kaifuku*
Alternative	*別の*	*Betsu no*
Coma	*昏睡*	*konsui*
Relax	*リラックス*	*rirakkusu*
Cure	*治す*	*naosu*
Chronic	*慢性*	*mansei*
Calcium	*カルシウム*	*karushiumu*
Defiant	*反抗的な*	*Hankouteki na*
Malnourishment	*栄養失調*	*Eiyou shicchou*
Treatment	*処理*	*shori*
Junk	*ジャンク*	*janku*
Appetite	*食欲*	*shokuyoku*
Biceps	*上腕二頭筋*	*Jouwan nitoukin*
Courage	*勇気*	*yuuki*

Vocabulary	Japanese	Transliteration
Doctor	医者	*Isha*
Bone	骨	*hone*
Inflammation	炎症	*enshou*
Insurance	保険	*hoken*
Longevity	長寿	*chouju*
Moisture	水分	*suibun*

Chapter 12: Seasons, days of the week and time

English Phrase	Japanese	Transliteration
Winter has arrived! (Expression)	*冬がやってきました！*	*Fuyu ga yatte kimashita!*
What is the temperature?	*何度ですか？*	*Nando desuka?*
The summer here is too hot!	*ここの夏は暑すぎる！*	*Kokono natsu wa atsusugiru!*
Where are you going in the spring holidays?	*春休みはどこに行きますか？*	*Haruyasumi wa doko ni ikimasuka?*
The snow was heavy	*雪は重かった*	*Yuki wa omokatta*
The beach was packed out	*ビーチは満員でした*	*Bi-chi wa man-in deshita*
The leaves fell off the tree	*葉が木から落ちた*	*Ha ga ki kara ochita*
Monday	*月曜日*	*Getsu youbi*
Tuesday	*火曜日*	*Ka youbi*
Wednesday	*水曜日*	*Sui youbi*
Thursday	*木曜日*	*Moku youbi*
Friday	*金曜日*	*Kin youbi*
Saturday	*土曜日*	*Do youbi*
Sunday	*日曜日*	*Nichi youbi*

English Phrase	Japanese	Transliteration
January	*一月*	*ichigatsu*
February	*二月*	*nigatsu*
March	*三月*	*sangatsu*
April	*四月*	*shigatsu*
May	*五月*	*gogatsu*
June	*六月*	*rokugatsu*
July	*七月*	*shichigatsu*
August	*八月*	*hachigatsu*
September	*九月*	*kugatsu*
October	*十月*	*juugatsu*
November	*十一月*	*Juuichigatsu*
December	*十二月*	*juunigatsu*
Autumn is my favorite time of the year	*秋は一年の中で一番好きな時期です*	*Aki wa ichinen no naka de ichiban sukina jiki desu*
It was foggy	*霧が深かった*	*Kiri ga fukakatta*

English Phrase	Japanese	Transliteration
The rainbow came out	虹が現れた	*Niji ga arawareta*
The tornado was dangerous	竜巻は危険でした	*Tatsumaki wa kiken deshita*
It was a humid day	湿度の高い日でした	*Shitsudo no takai hi deshita*
What did you think of the heat wave?	猛暑についてどう思いましたか？	*Mousho ni tsuite dou omoimashitaka?*
I loved the breeze	あのそよ風が好きだった	*Ano soyokaze ga suki datta*
A thunderstorm is coming! (Expression)	雷雨が近づいています！	*Raiu ga chikazuite imasu!*
The crops are dying	作物が枯れている	*Sakumotsu ga karete iru*
It's only a little drizzle!	ほんの霧雨だよ！	*Honno kirisame dayo!*
What time is it?	今何時？	*Ima nanji?*
It is one o'clock	1時です	*Ichiji desu*
It is two o'clock	2時です	*Niji desu*
It is three o'clock	3時です	*Sanji desu*
It is four o'clock	4時です	*Yoji desu*
It is five o'clock	5時です	*Goji desu*

English Phrase	Japanese	Transliteration
It is six o'clock	*6時です*	*Rokuji desu*
It is seven o'clock	*7時です*	*Shichiji desu*
It is eight o'clock	*8時です*	*Hachiji desu*
It is nine o'clock	*9時です*	*Kuji desu*
It is ten o'clock	*10時です*	*Juuji desu*
It is eleven o'clock	*11時です*	*Juuichiji desu*
It is twelve o'clock	*12時です*	*Juuniji desu*
The hour is going back tomorrow	*時間は明日に戻ります*	*Jikan wa ashita ni modorimasu*
Check the calendar	*カレンダーを見てください*	*Karenda- wo mite kudasai*
This decade went quick	*この10年はあっという間だった*	*Kono juunen wa atto iuma datta*
What are you doing next week?	*来週は何をしますか？*	*Raishuu wa nani wo shimasuka?*
How old are you?	*何歳ですか？*	*Nansai desuka?*
The clock is broken	*時計は壊れている*	*Tokei wa kowarete iru*
What is your time zone?	*あなたのタイムゾーンでは何時ですか？*	*Anata no taimuzo-n dewa nanji desuka?*

Chapter 12: Vocabulary

Vocabulary	Japanese	Transliteration
Winter	冬	*Fuyu*
Temperature	温度	*ondo*
Hot	熱い	*Atsui*
Spring	春	*haru*
Snow	冬	*fuyu*
Beach	ビーチ	*Bi-chi*
Leaves	葉	*ha*
Autumn	秋	*aki*
Foggy	霧深い	*kiribukai*
Rainbow	虹	*niji*
Tornado	竜巻	*tatsumaki*
Humid	湿気が多い	*Shikke ga ooi*
Wave	波	*nami*
Breeze	そよ風	*Soyokaze*

Vocabulary	Japanese	Transliteration
Thunderstorm	*雷雨*	*raiu*
Crops	*作物*	*sakumotsu*
Drizzle	*霧雨*	*kirisame*
Calendar	*カレンダー*	*Karena-*
Decade	*十年期*	*juunenki*
Broken	*壊れている*	*kowareteiru*
Time zone	*タイムゾーン*	*Taimuzo-n*

Chapter 13: Conversations

English Phrase	Japanese	Transliteration
It's been a while	お久しぶりです	*Ohisashiburi desu*
What have you been up to recently?	最近はどうしていましたか？	*Saikin wa doushite imashitaka?*
Things are going great!	良い感じだよ！	*Ii kanji dayo!*
Could be better	あまり良くないです	*Amari yoku naidesu*
I'm going through a difficult period	大変な時期ですね	*Taihen na jiki desune*
I need your help	助けてください	*Tasukete kudasai*
Same old! (Expression)	同い年です！	*Onaidoshi desu!*
Things are going really well	すごくいい感じです！	*Sugoku ii kanji desu!*
Thank you	ありがとう	*arigatou*
I appreciate that!	ありがとうございます！	*Arigatou gozaimasu!*
You are welcome	どういたしまして	*Douitashimashite*
Any time!	いつでもどうぞ！	*Itsudemo douzo!*
It's my pleasure	どういたしまして	*douitashimashite*
I agree	同意します	*Doui shimasu*

English Phrase	Japanese	Transliteration
I disagree	同意しません	*Doui shimasen*
Couldn't have said it better myself!	うまいこと言いますね！	*Umaikoto iimasune!*
That is so true!	その通り！	*Sono toori!*
That is not true	そんなことはありませんよ	*Sonna koto wa arimasen yo!*
Not necessarily	必ずしもそうではない	*Kanarazushimo sou dewa nai*
I have a meeting	会議があります	*Kaigi ga arimasu*
I'm running late	遅れそうです	*Okuresou desu*
Let's catch up later	また後でね	*Mata atode ne*
Pardon me; I have to take this call	すみません、電話にでなくちゃ	*Sumimasen, denwa ni denakucha*
That's so considerate of you	お気遣いありがとうございます	*Okizukai arigatou gozaimasu*
That has made my day	良い日になったよ	*Ii ichinichi ni nattayo*
I want to thank you from the bottom of my heart	心の底から感謝したい	*Kokoro no soko kara kansha shitai*
No sweat (Expression)	お安い御用です	*Oyasui goyou desu*
It is the least I can do	せめてそれくらいはさせてください	*Semete sorekurai wa sasete kudasai*

English Phrase	Japanese	Transliteration
It wasn't my fault	私のせいではなかったです	*Watashi no sei dewa nakatta desu*
It was my fault	私のせいです	*Watashi no sei desu*
I take full responsibility	全責任を負います	*Zen sekinin wo oimasu*
That shouldn't have happened	そんなことはあってはいけなかった	*Sonna kotowa attewa ikenakatta*
I hope you can forgive me for that	ご容赦頂ければ幸いです	*Goyousha itadakereba saiwai desu*
I owe you an apology	恩に着るよ	*On ni kiruyo*
That wasn't right	正しくはなかった	*Tadashikuwa nakatta*
I'm on cloud nine! (Expression)	とっても嬉しい！	*Tottemo ureshii!*
Could you spare a minute?	ちょっといいですか？	*Chotto iidesuka?*
Can I pick your brain? (expression)	お知恵を拝借させていただけませんか？	*Ochie wo haishaku sasete itadakemasenka?*
I can't hear you	聞こえません	*kikoemasen*
Come closer	こちらに来てください	*Kochira ni kite kudasai*
You're too far away	遠すぎます	*Toosugi masu*
Speak up a bit	もう少し大きな声でお願いします	*Mousukoshi ookina koe de onegai shimasu*

English Phrase	Japanese	Transliteration
Can we speak another time?	*また今度でもいいですか？*	*Mata kondo demo ii desuka?*
It was nice catching up	*話せてよかったよ*	*Hanasete yokattayo*
Give me a moment	*少々お待ちください*	*Shoushou omachi kudasai*
Can you pass on a message for me?	*伝言を承りましょうか？*	*Dengon wo uketamawarimashouka?*
How can I put it?	*どう言えばいいでしょうか*	*Dou ieba ii deshouka?*
Do you understand now?	*分かりましたか？*	*Wakarimashitaka?*
That doesn't make sense	*矛盾しています*	*Mujun shiteimasu*
I'm sick and tired of you! (Expression)	*うんざりです！*	*Unzari desu*
Stop beating around the bush! (Expression)	*回りくどい言い方はやめてくれ！*	*Mawarikudoi iikata wa yametekure!*
Can I have your details?	*詳細を教えていただけますか？*	*Shousai wo oshiete itadakemasuka?*
Is that your friend?	*あなたの友達ですか？*	*Anata no tomodachi desuka?*
Where can I find you?	*どちらでお会いできますか？*	*Dochira de oai dekimasuka?*
Take my business card	*私の名刺をお受け取りください*	*Watashi no meishi wo ouketori kudasai*
I'll be expecting a call later	*後程のご連絡をお待ちしております*	*Nochihodo no gorenraku wo omachishite orimasu*

English Phrase	Japanese	Transliteration
What languages do you speak?	*どの言語で話しますか？*	*Dono gengo de hanashi masuka?*
You speak very fast	*とても早く話しますね*	*totemo hayaku hanashimasune*
Are you sure about that?	*本当にこれでいいんですか？*	*Hontouni korede iindesuka?*
What if it goes wrong?	*間違っていたらどうしますか？*	*Machigatte itara doushimasuka?*
I can't take a chance	*チャンスを掴めません*	*Chansu wo tsukamemasen*
Can you double-check?	*再確認していただけますか？*	*Saikakunin shite itadakemasuka?*
I'm not a hundred percent sure	*100%の確信は持てません*	*Hyakupa-sento no kakushin wa motemasen*
I have my doubts	*疑わしくはあります*	*Utagawashiku wa arimasu*
That sounds stupid	*バカみたいですね*	*Baka mitai desune*
Why would you say that?	*どうしてそんなことを言うんですか？*	*Doushite sonna koto wo iundesuka?*
I don't think we have met?	*お会いしたことはないと思いますが？*	*Oai shita koto wa nai to omoimasu ga?*
There's nothing to be scared about	*恐れることはありません*	*Osoreru koto wa arimasen*
What are your thoughts on..	*…についてどう思いますか？*	*…ni tsuite dou omoimasuka?*
Rate it on a scale of one to ten	*1から10で表してください*	*Ichi kara juu de arawashite kudasai*

English Phrase	Japanese	Transliteration
I'd like to make you an offer	是非お願いしたいです	*Zehi onegai shitai desu*
I would like to accept	お受けいたします	*Ouke itashimasu*
I would like to reject	お断りさせてください	*Okotowari sasete kudasai*
Forgive me for my mistake	ご容赦のほどお願い申し上げます	*Goyousha no hodo onegai moushi agemasu*
Admittedly, I was wrong	確かに私が間違っていました	*Tashikani watashi ga machigatte imashita*
Let's join forces	力を合わせましょう	*Chikara wo awase mashou*
It looks that way	そうだと思います	*Souda to omoimasu*
I guess so	おそらくそうでしょう	*Osoraku soudeshou*
I hope you can consider	ご検討いただけますと幸いです	*Gokentou itadakemasuto saiwai desu*
Sleep on it (Expression)	時間を置いて考える	*Jikan wo oite kangaeru*
Think about it	考えてみてください	*Kangaete mitekudasai*
I would love to	是非そうしたいです	*Zehi sou shitai desu*
Could you clarify?	明確にしていただけますか？	*Meikaku ni shite itadakemasuka?*
Do you have any questions?	質問はありますか？	*Shitsumon wa arimasuka?*

English Phrase	Japanese	Transliteration
I have some good news	*良い知らせがあります*	*Ii shirase ga arimasu*
I have some bad news	*悪い知らせがあります*	*Warui shirase ga arimasu*
I'm happy to inform you..	*お知らせできて嬉しいです*	*Oshirase dekite ureshii desu*
I'm excited to inform you	*お知らせできることに興奮しています*	*Oshirase dekiru koto ni koufun shite imasu*
For real?	*本当に？*	*Hontou ni?*
Are you being serious?	*本気ですか？*	*Honki desuka?*
You can't be serious!	*冗談だろ！*	*Joudan daro!*
I can't believe it!	*信じられない！*	*Shinji rarenai!*
I'm sorry to hear that	*それは残念でしたね*	*Sore wa zannen deshitane*
I'm disappointed to hear that	*聞いてがっかりしました*	*Kiite gakkari shimashita*
That was the last thing I was expecting	*思いもよりませんでした*	*Omoimo yorimasen deshita*
That is a surprise	*驚きです*	*Odoroki desu*
I did not know that	*知りませんでした*	*Shirimasen deshita*
Why is that so?	*どうしてそんなことに？*	*Doushite sonna kotoni?*

English Phrase	Japanese	Transliteration
I'm a little nervous	*ちょっと緊張しています*	*Chotto kinchou shite imasu*
Sorry for the confusion	*混乱させてしまってごめんなさい*	*Konran sasete shimatte gomennasai*
That was not the intention	*そんなつもりではありませんでした*	*Sonna tsumori dewa arimasen deshita*
Take a seat	*お掛けください*	*Okake kudasai*
Pardon me	*すみません*	*sumimasen*
I'd like to introduce myself	*自己紹介させてください*	*Jikoshoukai sasete kudasai*
I'm sorry to hear that	*それは残念でしたね*	*Sorewa zannen deshitane*
Do you have any siblings?	*ご兄弟はいますか？*	*Gokyoudai wa imasuka?*
What is your line of work?	*お仕事は何をされているんですか？*	*Oshigoto wa nani wo sarete irundesuka?*
What country are you from?	*ご出身はどちらですか？*	*Goshusshin wa dochira desuka?*
Do you follow a religion?	*信仰はございますか？*	*Shinkou wa gozaimasuka?*
What state are you from?	*どちらの州の出身ですか？*	*Dochira no shuu no shusshin desuka?*
Not to my knowledge	*私の知る限りは違う*	*Watashi no shiru kagiri wa chigau*
How can you justify that?	*正当化できますか？*	*Seitouka dekimasuka?*

English Phrase	Japanese	Transliteration
I would love to accompany you	*是非お供させてください*	*Zehi otomo sasete kudasai*
Do you have a budget?	*予算はありますか？*	*Yosan wa arimasuka?*
I feel obliged	*義務感がある*	*Gimukan ga aru*
That's rare to see!	*滅多に見られません！*	*Metta ni miraremasen!*
You have the capability!	*あなたにはその能力があります！*	*Anata ni wa sono nouryoku ga arimasu!*
I would love to be in your position	*あなたの立場になりたい*	*Anata no tachiba ni naritai*
Let's talk elsewhere	*別の場所で話しましょう*	*Betsu no basho de hanashimashou*
This is an emergency	*緊急事態です*	*Kinkyuu jitai desu*
This is new to me	*それは初耳です*	*Sore wa hatsumimi desu*
I totally understand	*全部理解しています*	*Zenbu rikai shite imasu*
The matter is unclear	*内容が不透明です*	*Naiyou ga futoumei desu*
That is your view	*それはあなたの見解です*	*Sore wa anata no kenkai desu*
I can imagine	*想像できます*	*Souzou dekimasu*
What are the implications of that?	*それはどういった意味合いですか？*	*Sore wa douitta imiai desuka?*

English Phrase	Japanese	Transliteration
I would like to take you up on that offer	*お言葉に甘えて*	*Okotoba ni amaete*
Let me illustrate	*解説させてください*	*Kaisetsu sasete kudasai*
That was the highlight for me	*それが私にとってのハイライトでした*	*Sore ga watashi ni totteno hairaito deshita*
I would like to incorporate that into my schedule	*スケジュールに組み込ませてください*	*Sukeju-ru ni kumikomasete kudasai*
Ultimately, it comes down to..	*最終的には…でしょう*	*Saishuuteki niwa … deshou*
That's so cringe!	*とてもうんざりです！*	*Totemo unzari desu!*
That was satisfying	*満足でした*	*Manzoku deshita*
What a relief!	*ホッとした*	*Hotto shita*
I admire your manners	*礼儀正しくて感心します*	*Reigi tadashikute kanshin shimasu*
It took forever!	*時間がかかりすぎた*	*Jikanga kakari sugita*
It was only brief	*ほんの一瞬です*	*Honno isshun desu*
When can I expect a reply?	*いつまでにお返事をいただけますか？*	*Itsumade ni ohenji wo itadakemasuka?*
That's so funny!	*とても面白い！*	*Totemo omoshiroi!*
That's hilarious!	*とても楽しい！*	*Totemo tanoshii!*

English Phrase	Japanese	Transliteration
That was tremendous!	*すばらしかった！*	*Subarashikatta!*
In my opinion..	*私の意見としては…*	*Watashi no iken toshitewa...*
I wouldn't do that if I were you	*私があなたならそんなことはしませんよ*	*Watashi ga anata nara sonna koto wa shimasen yo*
That is confidential information	*それは機密情報です*	*Sore wa kimitsu jikou desu*
What's your email address?	*Eメールアドレスは何ですか？*	*i-me-ru adoresu wa nandesuka?*
Slow down a little	*ちょっと落ち着こう*	*Chotto ochitsukou*
Can we reserve a table for two?	*2人のテーブルを予約できますか？*	*Futari no te-buru wo yoyaku dekimasuka?*
I do apologize for the inconvenience	*ご不便をおかけして申し訳ございません*	*Gofuben wo okake shite mousiwake gozaimasen*
I need to think about it	*それについて検討する必要があります*	*Sore ni tsuite kentou suru hitsuyou ga arimasu*
It's hard to say	*何とも言い難い*	*Nantomo iigatai*
It depends..	*…によります*	*… ni yorimasu*
I have a feeling that's not true	*そうじゃない気がする*	*Sou janai kiga suru*
If I were to make a guess	*推測するなら*	*Suisoku suru nara*
That was unexpected	*予想外でした*	*Yosougai deshita*

English Phrase	Japanese	Transliteration
I'm absolutely convinced...	*…だと完全に確信している*	*… da to kanzen ni kakushin shiteiru*
The problem is that...	*問題は… です*	*Mondai wa … desu*
Of course, that's obvious	*もちろん、明らかにそうです*	*Mochiron, akirakani sou desu*
How dare you!	*よくもそんなことができるな！*	*Yokumo sonna kotoga dekiruna!*
Shame on you!	*恥を知れ！*	*Haji wo shire!*
Undoubtedly so	*間違いなくそう*	*Machigainaku sou*
From another angle...	*別の角度から見れば*	*Betsu no kakudo kara mireba*
Let me see what I can do for you	*やれるだけのことはやってみます*	*Yareru dake no koto wa yatte mimasu*
You've got to be kidding me! (Expression)	*冗談でしょ！*	*Joudan desho!*
You owe me one	*ひとつ貸しだよ*	*Hitotsu kashi dayo*
Fair enough	*君の言うとおりだ*	*Kimi no iu toori da*
Why are you so sad? Cheer up!	*何を悲しんでいるんだ？元気出せよ！*	*Nani wo kanashinde irunda? Genki daseyo!*
Let's leave it at that	*この辺にしておこう*	*Kono hen ni shite okou*
Back in my day...	*当時は…*	*Touji wa...*

English Phrase	Japanese	Transliteration
I've been there and done that! (Expression)	*私も同じ経験をしたよ！*	*Watashi mo onaji keiken wo shita yo!*
Better late than never (Expression)	*やらないよりはやったほうがいい*	*Yaranai yori wa yatta houga ii*
Keep this between you and me	*ここだけの話*	*Kokodake no hanashi*
I haven't got a clue! (Expression)	*全然わからない！*	*Zenzen wakaranai!*
Time to rise and shine! (Expression)	*起きる時間だよ！*	*Okiru jikan dayo!*
How do you know?	*どうしてわかったの？*	*Doushite wakatta no?*
What's the big deal?	*だから何？*	*Dakara nani?*
Who cares anyway?	*誰も気にしないよ*	*Daremo kini shinai yo*
You would be better off not to..	*…しないほうがいい*	*… shinai houga ii*
I would have never dreamt of that	*夢にも思わなかった*	*Yume nimo omowanakatta*
Never in a million years! (Expression)	*絶対あり得ない！*	*Zettai arienai!*
Who asked you that?	*誰に頼まれたんですか？*	*Dare ni tanomaretandesuka?*
Mark my words (Expression)	*よく聞いて*	*Yoku kiite*
Enough is enough! (Expression)	*いい加減にして！*	*Iikagen ni shite!*

Chapter 13: Vocabulary

Vocabulary	Japanese	Transliteration
Recently	最近	*Saikin*
Period	期間	*Kikan*
Pardon	すみません	*sumimasen*
Forgive	許す	*yurusu*
Apology	ごめんなさい	*Gomen nasai*
Brain	脳	*nou*
Card	カード	*Ka-do*
Language	言語	*gengo*
Accept	受ける	*ukeru*
Reject	拒否	*kyohi*
Offer	オファー	*Ofa-*
Mistake	間違い	*machigai*
Consider	検討	*kentou*
Clarify	明らかにする	*Akiraka ni suru*

Vocabulary	Japanese	Transliteration
Disappointed	*残念だった*	*Zannen datta*
Surprise	*驚く*	*odoroku*
Confusion	*混乱する*	*Konran suru*
Intention	*目的*	*mokuteki*
Seat	*シート*	*Shi-to*
Introduce	*紹介*	*shoukai*
Religion	*信仰*	*shinkou*
State	*州*	*shuu*
Knowledge	*知識*	*chishiki*
Justify	*正当化する*	*seitouka*
Budget	*予算*	*yosan*
Rare	*珍しい*	*mezurashii*
Capability	*容量*	*youryou*
Position	*位置*	*ichi*

Vocabulary	Japanese	Transliteration
Emergency	*緊急*	*kinkyuu*
Imagine	*想像する*	*Souzou suru*
Implications	*暗示する*	*Anji suru*
Illustrate	*説明する*	*Setsumei suru*
Highlight	*ハイライト*	*hairaito*
Cringe	*すくむ*	*sukumu*
Satisfying	*満足*	*manzoku*
Relief	*安心*	*anshin*
Manners	*マナー*	*Mana-*
Brief	*短い*	*mijikai*
Funny	*面白い*	*omoshiroi*
Hilarious	*陽気な*	*youkina*
Tremendous	*絶大*	*zetsudai*
Opinion	*意見*	*iken*

Vocabulary	Japanese	Transliteration
Convinced	*確信している*	*Kakushin shiteiru*
Obvious	*明らか*	*akiraka*
Angle	*角度*	*kakudo*
Kidding	*冗談*	*joudan*

Chapter 14: Expressions

Expression	Japanese	Transliteration
You've hit the nail on the head there	*まさにその通り*	*Masani sono toori*
Let's catch up soon	*またお会いしましょう*	*Mata oai shimashou*
There's plenty of fish in the sea	*相手なんて他にいくらでもいるよ*	*Aite nante hoka ni ikurademo iruyo*
That's the spirit!	*その調子！*	*Sono choushi!*
I am over the moon!	*嬉しくてたまらないよ！*	*Ureshikute tamaranaiyo!*
I am dying of rage!	*死ぬほど腹が立つ！*	*Shinu hodo haraga tatsu!*
Don't sweat it!	*心配するな！*	*Shinpai suruna!*
The game went down to the wire	*試合は最後まで接戦でした*	*Shiai wa saigo made sessen deshita*
Prevention is better than cure	*予防は治療に勝る*	*Yobou wa chiryou ni masaru*
Victory is ours!	*我々の勝利だ！*	*Wareware no shouri da!*
It's your time to shine!	*あなたが輝く時ですよ！*	*Anata ga kagayaku toki desuyo!*
Winter has arrived!	*冬がやってきた！*	*Fuyu ga yattekita!*
A thunderstorm is coming!	*雷雨が近づいてきます！*	*Raiu ga chikazuite kimasu!*
Same old!	*同い年だ！*	*Onaidoshi da!*

Expression	Japanese	Transliteration
No sweat	*お安い御用です*	*Oyasui goyou desu*
I'm on cloud nine!	*とっても嬉しい！*	*Tottemo ureshii!*
Can I pick your brain?	*お知恵を拝借させていただけませんか？*	*Ochie wo haishaku sasete itadakemasenka?*
I'm sick and tired of you!	*うんざりです！*	*Unzaridesu!*
Stop beating around the bush!	*回りくどい言い方はやめてくれ！*	*Mawarikudoi iikata wa yamete kure!*
Sleep on it	*時間を置いて考える*	*Jikan wo oite kangaeru*
You've got to be kidding me!	*冗談でしょ！*	*Joudan desho!*
I've been there and done that!	*私も同じ経験をしたよ！*	*Watashi mo onaji keiken wo shitayo!*
Better late than never	*やらないよりはやったほうがいい*	*Yaranai yoriwa yatta houga ii*
I haven't got a clue!	*全然わからない！*	*Zenzen wakaranai!*
Time to rise and shine!	*起きる時間だよ！*	*Okiru jikan dayo!*
Never in a million years!	*絶対あり得ない！*	*Zettai arienai!*
Mark my words	*よく聞いて*	*Yoku kiite*
Enough is enough!	*いい加減にして！*	*Iikagen ni shite!*

Conclusion

Thank you for purchasing and completing this phrasebook.

I hope that you have found the content fruitful and beneficial.

Please remember that you will only become fluent after a period of time, especially with a language like Japanese, which is on the harder side of languages.

You will need to stay consistent with your revision, and once you have become confident with the words and phrases in this book, I recommend you study a curriculum that teaches you the basics of grammar. This will allow you to construct sentences that are grammatically correct and eloquent.

Please understand that this is only the beginning of your studies if you want to take this language seriously and reach a native level.

You will need to do significantly more self-study and attend classroom classes to reach a level of a native.

www.ingramcontent.com/pod-product-compliance
Ingram Content Group UK Ltd.
Pitfield, Milton Keynes, MK11 3LW, UK
UKHW061830190726
13853UKWH00009B/2532